The Second Bird-watchers' Book

The Second Bird-watchers' Book

Compiled and Edited by
JOHN GOODERS

DAVID & CHARLES

NEWTON ABBOT   LONDON
NORTH POMFRET (VT)   VANCOUVER

ISBN 0 7153 7047 2

Library of Congress Catalog Card Number 75-10531
© John Gooders 1975

Set in 11 on 13pt Imprint
and printed in Great Britain
by Latimer Trend & Company Ltd Plymouth
for David & Charles (Holdings) Limited
South Devon House Newton Abbot Devon

Published in the United States of America
by David & Charles Inc
North Pomfret Vermont 05053 USA

Published in Canada
by Douglas David & Charles Limited
132 Philip Avenue North Vancouver BC

Contents

after the impossible. This is his story—the search for
the most rare and most difficult subjects on which to
train his lenses

Illustrations

All the photographs in this book have been supplied by Ardea Photographics, except those on pp 89 (*bottom*), 90 (*top and bottom*) and 107 (*top*).

Introduction

Such was the reception of the first *Bird-watchers' Book* when it appeared in 1974 that plans were immediately put into action to produce this second edition. Once again the aim was to get the top men to write about their own speciality in a readable and enjoyable way, a way that everyone (even including scientists) could understand. Once more a glance through the list of contributors should convince anyone that we have succeeded.

In an age in which the pace is set by the television interview, where every second must be fully employed, even if the result is unsatisfactory and perfunctory, it is the function of the written word to enable ideas to be expanded and stories to be told in full. Much modern literature is overgeared to the same TV idiom and the design of the spread may take precedence over the ideas to be expressed. Perhaps the nicest thing about our formula is that we seldom tie our writers to a definite length. If they feel that the subject needs more space they just go ahead and write what is required. The result, we feel, is a fully coherent expression of the work of our experts.

In this entirely new edition of *The Bird-watchers' Book* the expertise and skill of professional and amateur are brought together to cover, once more, a vast range of subjects. Several articles, like those of Mike Harris and Bryan Nelson, summarise a wealth of papers that have appeared in ornithological journals widely scattered in time and space. Others, like that of Derrick England, tell stories that have long fascinated bird-watchers, but which have never before been told. The aim throughout has been to produce variety without losing sight of the need to link subjects in some, albeit tenuous, way. Thus it is no coincidence that most of the contributors are drawn from the British Trust for Ornithology and the Zoology Department of the University of Aberdeen, two of the 'hothouses' of British ornithology.

The Bird-watchers' Book is now established as compulsory fare for British bird-watchers. Already we are planning a third edition, seeking out the experts who will make a contribution to your fireside bird-watching and an invaluable addition to your bookshelf. The first edition is still available, but if you find difficulty in obtaining it the publishers will be pleased to help. For though *The Bird-watchers' Book* will appear regularly it is quite dateless and each version will be a source of pleasure and information for years to come.

London 1975   J.G.

Bird protection— the next five years

Peter Conder

Bird protection in the last five years has expanded vigorously. The amount of land set aside for bird reserves, chiefly by the voluntary bodies, has increased; holdings of the Royal Society for the Protection of Birds alone have increased from around 15,000 acres in 1969 to approximately 30,000 at the end of 1974. The government's Nature Conservancy Council reviewed its priorities and only areas of great priority were established as nature reserves. The involvement of ordinary people has increased. The RSPB has continued to double its membership every three years, a process which began in 1960. By the end of 1974 the membership was 180,000. Other organisations in nature conservation, such as the County Trusts, have also grown in strength. The broader field of nature education and information has seen strides too. The magazine *Birds* continues to interest and inform. *Birds of the World*, a part-work, involved a new public. The press has, by and large, continued or even slightly increased its interest in nature and birds, particularly in bird stories, although it may have got bored with pollution, environment and (so we are told) conservation in the broad sense.

Thus, the record of the last five years provides a good springboard for those concerned with the protection of birds to move into the next five with vigilance and enterprise. What the future holds for our natural environment and our national heritage is impossible to foresee with accuracy. Who can foretell the effects of inflation on our economy and then upon our own pockets, upon which the voluntary bird-protection effort ultimately depends? As I write, land prices which have been growing frighteningly high have stabilised and may be falling. If we had any money, land should be easier to buy. But, unless the world population is stabilised or even reduced, the need for land for agriculture, or for other forms of industrial exploitation and housing, will intensify.

Wait for the Millennium?

The bird protector must moderate the damage caused by this agricultural and industrial use and, in view of the shortness of time, must operate on as broad a front as possible: educate, inform, persuade, acquire the freehold of land, and so on. Ideally, we would like to proselytise so that everyone became a conservationist—so that, when the industrialist was looking at the shoreline, for instance, he would say automatically that this section of the coast is too beautiful and too interesting scientifically to be used as a site for oil-platform construction, even though, from the point of view of cost and so on, it is ideal; or the naturalist would say that the industrial process is so important for the welfare of the country that the scientific interest must be sacrificed. What's good for the goose is good for the gander! But we may have to wait for the millennium for all that to happen.

The future may hold a big industrial slump but, with good government, this should only be a temporary setback which need not seriously affect the growth of the voluntary bodies, provided they can withstand increasing costs. I am always surprised that slumps normally do not slow membership growth or even, so far as the RSPB is concerned, the sale of its goods. 1975 should see the enrolment of the 200,000th member and, by 1980, we should be near the half-million mark. We shall certainly set that as our target—assuming that our main interest will remain in birds, even though in the educational field that is a limiting restriction.

Broader Interests

Of course, the membership may broaden their interest to move away from birds. This is possible for two reasons. Some people may get tired of ticking off bird lists and turn to longer lists of plants. Others may become more interested in ecology or the study of the birds' environment or their behaviour and, for that reason too, turn to plants and other forms of life. The problem of twitchers or list-tickers is that they are sometimes ignorant of bird biology and ecology and the interest to be found once they have crossed the identification barrier. They do not start asking themselves the questions that a naturalist normally asks. Twitchers can't get over the identification barrier.

The main task will be to protect birds on as broad a front as possible, with special campaigns on particular problems from time to time. As I suggested earlier, the chief basic problem facing birds is the growth of human population intermingled or entangled with selfishness. We want economic growth planned so that we can enjoy the material things of life which sustain us physically as well as the beautiful creations of nature, which console us spiritually. If we were to overcome this selfishness within the next five years, perhaps we might be able to do without the buying of land and concentrate on information and education, but that is a forlorn hope. Our

15

priorities must therefore be to acquire the freehold of land of first-class ornithological importance, and educate, inform and persuade.

Devolution

To develop its resources and generally to perform more effectively, and particularly to influence local authorities both in planning and education, the RSPB will be decentralising its functions and giving more power to the regions, although of course the very terms of its Charter mean that power must ultimately remain with its elected Council. Regional Officers have been established for many years in Scotland, Northern Ireland and Wales; in England, the first Regional Office was established in the north two years ago, and in 1974, offices were set up in the south-west and the south-east of England. A further four will be established in the next four years, their prime purpose being to maintain close contact with local authorities, particularly planning authorities. Ultimately it is hoped that a Regional Officer will be assisted by other executive staff. One outposted RSPB Education Officer will be appointed each year for the next ten years.

This decentralisation is inevitable in view of the Society's growth. Originally I had hoped that the merger with County Trusts would have provided a logical basis for our work, but it was not to be. What the RSPB is now doing will be done in such a way that it would not conflict with the possibilities of a merger. Nor is the RSPB competing with other bodies; there is enough to be done in the whole field of nature conservation without the various voluntary bodies falling over each other.

Reserve Functions

The owning of land by a voluntary bird-protection body has

Page 17 (*above*) Symbol of protective success—the Osprey has returned to breed in Scotland under the watchful eye of the RSPB; (*below*) a Black-tailed Godwit at its nest on the Ouse Washes. Once a closely guarded secret, the growth in power of the RSPB has ensured that large areas of the Washes have been purchased as nature reserves

Page 18 Persecuted by the misinformed, the Golden Eagle still manages to cling to many of its Scottish strongholds and has recently returned to breed in the English Lake District

several purposes. Not only does it safeguard a place of ornithological importance but, often in planning eyes, it can guard
a 'buffer' area around it: planners will not want to put something incongruous next door to a nature reserve. Furthermore,
a large number of people will want to come to a reserve, so it
has an educational function and a potential for spiritual re-
freshment. We need as much land as we can purchase to safeguard habitats, not only for our native breeding species, but
for those which usually fly west to winter in Britain. Provision
of winter habitat is beginning to feature more and more in our
thoughts, highlighted by events at Maplin Sands; pressures on
our estuaries for land reclamation, water storage and recreation
facilities are increasing fast and, if allowed to proceed un-
checked or without provision for alternative sites, could affect
the population of winter-visiting species. The drought in the
Sahel, south of the Sahara, has had disastrous effects, not only
on the human population, but also on our summer populations
of Whitethroat and Sand Martin, as well as other species; it
has shown the importance of wintering areas to birds so
familiar to us in summer.

Education

We need to educate, influence and persuade as many people
as possible of the 'rightness' of our cause, of its interest and
spiritual value. The next five years will see an intensification
of the RSPB's effort in school education in the field of birds
and their place in nature, both from headquarters and the
regions. The outposted Regional Officer will be liaising
closely with local education authorities and teachers, will
provide local courses for them and generally help conservation
education within his region. The headquarters hopes to produce more materials that teachers can use in field and class-

room. We need to stimulate the interest, too, of the 15–21 year-old. The Young Ornithologists' Club has a membership of 60,000 youngsters between the ages of 11 and 14, and now we are aiming to produce material for the older age-group, who have such agile, adult minds and often become super-intellectual. Young people tend to leave the YOC at the age of 13, but although they then become interested in other things such as boyfriends or girlfriends, we believe that they could continue to think about feathered birds too, provided the latter are made interesting.

Another problem that needs solving is that of the fairly new bird-watchers who do not get beyond the identification stage: here we need a big education campaign to persuade or to encourage people to ask themselves the question why?—why is that bird behaving this way, why is it eating that? Perhaps we need a campaign to show people how they should answer that question. This could enormously increase the interest in birds. Perhaps the leaders of bird clubs, RSPB members groups, and others could introduce courses on bird biology, particularly since there are now some good books on bird behaviour and biology which could stimulate interest in the same way that the first edition of James Fisher's book *Watching Birds* interested people during and after the last war.

Creating Naturalists

Bird identification is a stage in the bird-watcher's development—perhaps even a fashion, in the same way that the interest in territory and life-histories was a fashion just after the war. Then everybody studied visible migration, but new techniques using radar took the study of bird movements away from the amateur. The study of population seems to have died a natural death, and the study of bird behaviour, so far as amateurs were concerned, was killed by technical terms. So, in the next five years, we need to teach people how to become good naturalists—to have a discriminating affection for birds. A general love of birds is all very well, but one must appreciate that some species, such as Woodpigeons and Bullfinches, have harmful side-effects; these facts one must accept and, where necessary, be prepared for sacrifice. Bird protectors must sort the good from the bad, know when to fight and when to concede. Knowing something about the bird's reaction to its environment leads one to learning something about threats to man's environment: birds taught us about the dangers of organochlorine pesticides.

It is in this field that local bird clubs and a developing network of RSPB Members' Groups have a role. Bird clubs have a scientific role of reporting, as well as an educational role equivalent to that of RSPB Members' Groups. I would commend here the network research of the British Trust for Ornithology which harnesses, in a scientific way, the work of amateurs and which produces results for conservation. Once over the elementary hurdles, more amateurs could help the BTO with interesting and valuable projects.

Trade Unions

One problem always perplexes me—why doesn't the RSPB appeal to the upper class? Quite clearly it has a largely middle-class membership. Is it true that the upper class kills birds and the lower class cages them, while the middle class conserves them? Some big landowners farm and shoot and argue they are the best conservationists, forgetting the poletraps for owls that embellish some estates. Killing pheasants for eating isn't bad, though it has some considerable side-effects. But if landowners should stop shooting, what would happen to the game coverts and copses that shelter so many birds? Perhaps they would be turned into cornfields, arable land which generally provides a poor home for birds. Maybe we can influence these landowners more, as the National Trust has done, by becoming more involved with their properties, in such a way that they understand what bird protectors are really aiming at. What of the trade unions? Is there any chance in the next five years of persuading them to give thought to their environment as well as to money matters?

There has been much talk of people's involvement with planning. Bird protectors are becoming more and more involved too. With other ornithological bodies we found we had experience of problems relating to oil exploitation in Scotland and elsewhere. We must seek wherever we can to ensure that planning officers are aware of our position, so that their judgements and plans will be based on full knowledge of the scientific facts. This will be an increasing role of the RSPB Regional Officers to become established within the next four years.

Internationalism

Birds know no frontiers. The work of the ICBP has also established that close liaison is possible between national sections in relation to their governments. It is likely that the new European laws could ultimately affect legislation in this country, and EEC countries may seek closer co-operation than is at present provided for by European national sections of the ICBP. Indeed, within the next five years a reorganisation of the ICBP might become necessary. It has functioned well over many years and it is time that its relationship to the EEC was fundamentally examined. Whether closer ties with the International Union for the Conservation of Nature, which are already established through the special working parties into endangered bird species, will lead to a merger that some have suggested remains to be seen. This could lead to a loss of efficiency so far as birds and bird protection are concerned.

The ICBP works to governments, but national bodies, such as the RSPB, work with comparable national bodies. Week-long courses for staff of comparable voluntary bodies in the Netherlands, Germany, Turkey, Switzerland, Malta and Cyprus have been held at Sandy in the last three years and will, no doubt, continue to be a feature of the RSPB's work in the international field, helping towards a closer link between us all. Similar exchange visits are already regularly arranged between ourselves and nature conservationists in the United States.

In the next five years there is an enormous amount of work to be done over a wide field. Plans are laid. Finance must be found. The RSPB and other bodies like it must harness all their resources, their energy, their enterprise and their initiative in combating and solving the problems, so that the bird-watchers and naturalists who follow us have places in which they can see birds, appreciate their beauty of plumage and song, and learn to understand their wonderful adaptations and their place in nature.

The trade in wild birds

John A. Burton

A quick glance at the bird-keeper's newspaper, *Cage and Aviary Birds*, shows that the trade in captured wild birds is flourishing. Although the trade in native British birds is very strictly controlled (it is restricted to captive-bred specimens for most species) there are virtually no controls on caught wild birds imported from anywhere else in the world. The only group of exotic species to receive any real protection are the birds of prey (including owls): since 1970 licences have been needed to import all birds of prey, and although smuggling does occur quite frequently, there can be little doubt that the overall trade in these birds has been effectively reduced. Some other birds are afforded varying degrees of control under bits of legislation designed to prevent the spread of disease; these include species related to domestic fowl (pheasants etc) and waterfowl. Import of the plumage of some species is controlled (birds of paradise, egrets, etc) but not if it is on a living bird! For the vast majority of exotic species imported into Britain there is no adequate protection.

How Many Birds?

There are three main aspects of the trade to be considered:

the quantity, the quality (ie which species) and the conditions. The first is difficult, if not impossible, to assess at present, the second and third aspects can be studied more readily. The condition of the birds arriving in Britain has been commented on from time to time by officials of the RSPCA, who maintain a hostel for animals arriving at London's Heathrow Airport. Not infrequently reports appear in the press of horrific cases of ill-treatment of consignments of wild birds passing through the airport. The RSPCA's records are among the few reliable sources of information on the international trade in wild animals, but only about half the birds passing through London Airport are handled by the RSPCA, the rest going direct to the dealers. On this basis, probably something around 150,000 to 200,000 wild birds a year pass through London Airport. But this is only one point of entry (admittedly the most important); other airports also handle birds, and smaller numbers arrive by land and sea.

Mortality Rates

Bird dealers often claim that the mortality rate for imported birds is low—somewhere in the region of 2½ per cent dead on arrival. For some species the figure is much lower—for others (such as hummingbirds) very much higher. An average of 2½ per cent may sound quite low, but put into perspective, it is alarmingly high. Of 200,000 birds a year, 2½ per cent is 5,000 dead at London Airport alone, the only airport with any facilities for handling birds. The mortality recorded by an airport only represents a (unknown) fraction of the total mortality of the wild caught birds. When the birds are trapped there is often a high mortality involved in the actual capture; the trapper will then usually keep them until he has enough to sell to a dealer, and in the first few days after capture the death rate is often high. After passing through the hands of various middlemen an exporter will gather together a consignment, often housed under crowded, insanitary conditions, until there are sufficient or until an order comes in from abroad. Once the birds are in the hands of the importer the story continues. During the week or so immediately after importation mortality rates are often extremely high, and as they are passed from importer to the various dealers further deaths occur, particularly with tropical species not yet acclimatised. Eventually a retailer sells them to the bird-keeper. Even now with considerably more care and attention being lavished on the birds than at any other time in their captive existence, many die. If this were not so the importers would soon be out of business.

Although the International Air Transport Association (IATA) has laid down standards for the carriage of birds and other animals, in many cases these are disregarded. The birds are often crammed in small boxes without sufficient ventilation, food or water, and the slightest delay during the journey can result in mass deaths. The actual airflight is a very short proportion of the birds' life in captivity, and so a mortality of $2\frac{1}{2}$ per cent almost certainly only represents the tip of an iceberg. Apart from regular overcrowding, failure to provide food and water is one of the most frequent occurrences, but there are also 'horror stories' from time to time; one widely reported concerned a consignment of eagles which arrived at London Airport with the remains of parakeets scattered around their cage, and one live parakeet cowering in the water dish. The exporter had put the live parakeets in the cage to give the eagles food for the journey.

Who is to be blamed for this? I think quite clearly the blame can be laid on the British pet dealers. As long as they continue to accept birds sent under apalling conditions, then the dealers in Hong Kong, Singapore, Bangkok etc, will continue to send them. The cheapness of the birds is also an important factor: while many small birds are costing less than a pound a pair, the dealers can write off a large number and still make a clear profit.

And while dealers in Britain are unscrupulous enough to accept birds which they know have been deliberately smuggled from their country of origin, or are accompanied by forged licences, or licences obtained by bribes, then smuggling and poaching too will flourish. At every opportunity the Pet Trade Association (PTA) will state that it is only a handful of dealers who give the rest a bad name, but the PTA has made little attempt to curtail the activities of its members in this direction; it clearly requires a joint effort by all the dealers in wild animals to stamp out such activities.

The Variety Imported

As mentioned earlier, *Cage and Aviary Birds* gives a good idea of the variety of birds being imported. The advertisements include flamingoes, hummingbirds, tanagers, birds of paradise, parrots and large numbers of small species, as well as species listed by the IUCN as rare and endangered, and species protected in their country of origin. A considerable number of countries do in fact have comprehensive legislation designed to regulate and control the export of wildlife. But, particularly in the case of the underdeveloped nations, enforcement of the law can be difficult. Even the production of an export licence is no guarantee of legal export—all too often these can be acquired by bribery or forged (this was clearly demonstrated in the USA when leopard-skin coats were restricted).

TABLE I

Maximum prices of birds as advertised in *Cage and Aviary Birds*,
Oct 1974

Species	Price
Australian King Parrot (male)	£300
Pileated Parrot (male)	£175
Portlincoln Parrot (male)	£325
Barraband's Parrot (pair)	£165
Twenty-eight Parrot (male)	£275
Wrinkler Hornbill (pair)	£175
Greater Triton Cockatoo (female)	£70
Victoria Crowned Pigeons (4 pairs)	£800
Chilean Flamingoes (6 pairs)	£720
Humboldt's Penguins (6 pairs)	£960
White Pelicans (2 pairs)	£480
Inca Terns (4 pairs)	£200
Rhinoceros Hornbill (1)	£120
Red-fronted Macaw (1)	£480
'Barbets, unknown species, very rare'	£20
Hummingbirds (50)	£750

The high prices commanded by some species make the
risks involved in smuggling—should the species concerned be
protected—well worth taking. Many of the Australian
parrots advertised are captive-bred, but when they fetch
prices of £100 or more there is a strong incentive to export
them illegally. Parrots are not the only birds to be exported
illegally. During a four-year period, over 200 crowned
pigeons passed through the hands of the RSPCA at London's
Heathrow Airport—possibly representing nearer 500 actually
passing through the airport—and crowned pigeons are endemic in the Papuan region where permits are needed for the
export of wildlife. Crowned pigeons can be, and are, bred in
captivity, but only in small numbers.

TABLE 2
Species of crowned pigeons bred in captivity in 1972

Species	Zoo	Number bred
Goura cristata	Berlin	2
	Djakarta	2
	Pittsburgh	1
	Sao Paulo	1
	Seattle	1
	Surabaja	1
	Tampa	2
	Wassenaar	1
Goura scheepmakeri	Frankfurt	1
	Tampa	1
Goura victoria	Arnhem	1
	Bristol	1
TOTAL	11 ZOOS	15

In 1972, according to *The International Zoo Yearbook*, eleven zoos bred the three species of crowned pigeons (Table 2), producing a total of only fifteen young. The only zoo which is recorded as having bred from captive-bred stock was Sydney, but the young did not survive. Most zoos and bird gardens are apparently quite prepared to pay around £200 a pair, on the open market, for captured wild specimens. Nearly all zoos purchase, and have on show, birds and other animals which were probably illegally exported from their native country—one assumes that this is usually done in ignorance, but that is no excuse.

Legislation and its Effects

In 1973, under the auspices of the IUCN, a convention was signed in Washington which was designed to control the trade in endangered wildlife. Although many nations signed, by the end of 1974 only a handful had actually ratified; obviously a nation cannot do so until it has the necessary internal legislation to enforce the convention—which becomes operative after ten nations have ratified, but by the time this book is published there is little doubt that an Endangered Species Act will have been passed by the British parliament, and that it will set up the machinery needed to control the trade in rare birds. Additionally, signatory nations agree to co-operate in enforcing national legislation, even if the species concerned are not considered to be rare on a worldwide basis.

The ultimate aim of the bird-conservation movement should be severely to restrict all trade in wild-caught birds, and to ensure that the conditions under which any that may be sold are kept and transported are above any possible criticism.

Effects of Restrictions on the Pet Trade

The vast majority of birds can be bred in captivity—and in fact an extremely wide variety have been bred over the years. Captive-bred birds are pre-adapted to a captive environment and should be more attractive to the genuine aviculturist. However the 'fancier' who merely exhibits birds in cage-bird exhibitions finds it less costly (both in time and cash) to purchase wild birds. These are probably the only people who would suffer from the imposition of strict controls on the trade in captured wild birds. The dealers and breeders would continue in business, but with captive-bred specimens, commanding higher prices and offering a steadier return due to much-reduced mortality.

The rare and the difficult

M. D. England

Birds may be difficult to photograph for many reasons: because they are wary and notoriously averse to facing a hide; because they inhabit remote or inaccessible places or nest in difficult sites such as tall trees, high cliffs or impassable swamps; or because they are rare and hard to locate.

A psychologist would answer the question, 'Why is it that some people simply must rise to the bait of a job which has defeated other people or is especially difficult?' in unflattering terms, and would include references to inferiority complexes. Be that as it may I am, so far as senility will permit, an unrepentant searcher after the difficult or the 'un-done', and find that the less the challenge the poorer the performance. Although opportunities to join a party going to a place to photograph whatever birds turned up are not to be spurned, I am not much good at it, being only at my best when I must be single-minded, resisting temptations to raise the nose from the grindstone.

The successful photographing of a rare or difficult bird (usually abroad) unless it happens by sheer luck—as it never seems to do to me—involves an amount of preparation and research which may surprise the uninitiated.

Research

Preparation consists of reading—searching through all the relevant literature about the chosen species; and writing—to everyone who may be able to advise on where, when and how, to landowners, governments, even ambassadors (who in my experience can be incredibly helpful). One is often tempted to revile one's fellow-countrymen for their dilatory habits in answering letters; experience soon teaches one that the average Englishman is a model in this respect compared with his friends on the Continent. I think the first prize for failure to answer letters should go to Norway, with Denmark—rather surprisingly—following closely. Perhaps, on reflection, the prize should go outright to the Portuguese. I hasten to add that I have, chiefly as a result of bird trips, very good friends in each of these countries, who have given me a quite extraordinary amount of help and who are always sincerely apologetic about the delays. But they will nevertheless take another six months and three or four reminders before they answer my next letter. The trouble is that so often the next move cannot be made until one is reasonably certain about the one before. One cannot, for example, write to a landowner until one is told who he is, and a party cannot be invited until it is known when and where they will be going.

Black-winged Kite

Let us illustrate the general method with a particular case: the black-winged kite. For some years it had been increasingly apparent that the noncommittal attitude of field guides and other books to the status of this bird in Europe was unsatisfactory and was based on an almost complete lack of information. 'South-west Europe—may nest'; 'Possibly breeds Portugal': 'Said to occur Portugal' are pretty useless to serious students of ornithology, but could hardly be bettered as stimulants.

Searching the literature was unrewarding. The author of the only book on Portuguese birds apparently knew of one nest only, over forty years before. Descriptions of favoured habitats and nesting sites in books about these birds in other parts of the world—the species is very widespread—not only did not help, but were in the event frankly misleading so far as Portugal was concerned. Even caves were suggested as nest sites (subsequently shown to be confusion with Egyptian vultures) and there seemed to be practically no type of terrain where they were not to be found. Most insisted that they were primarily crepuscular. In fact I have seen them in the heat of the day on roadside telegraph wires in Africa, in remote open forest in India, and hunting at midday over a goods-yard in Melbourne. Apart from the caves already mentioned, nests were said to be always in trees and fairly high ones at that.

The Portuguese 'Forestry Commission'—ever helpful, as has subsequently been proved, apart from an almost patho-logical reluctance to set pen to paper—knew nothing of the bird except that one was occasionally reported as shot in winter. Those few landowners (both British and Portuguese) who replied to letters of inquiry were unable to give useful information, but the greatest good fortune put me in touch with an Englishman living in Oporto who had in his possession the notes of a long-dead egg-collector who described the nests of two black-winged kites and even named the locality. (Little imagination was needed to envisage the fate of the eggs.) The owner of the estate not only replied to a letter but gave permission for us to do what we liked and to make use of his keeper.

Portuguese Invasion

A party was chosen and an invasion of Portugal planned for the following year. Three cars would be needed, two to be driven from home, one to be hired on site.

We had no helpers on the spot (although a Portuguese ornithologist and some representatives of the Forestry Commission visited us while we were there) and so it was decided that one member should precede the main party by a week to reconnoitre and find somewhere for us to live. No less a person than the then Curator of Birds for the Zoological Society of London volunteered for this job, and ideal he proved to be. By the time we arrived he had not only found a suitable *pensao* where we could stay, but the whole village was alerted to help. He had recruited a retired minister of religion as interpreter and, without knowing a word of Portuguese, had established a friendly liaison with all and sundry.

After settling in, two of us plus interpreter set out to find the estate and introduce ourselves to the keeper, who proved friendly but unhelpful since, although he claimed to know the 'white hawk', he had not seen one for many years. However, not to be outdone, he led us on that and many subsequent days from one belt of high trees to another, ever looking upward (he assured us that the nest would be high) until his enthusiasm for an apparently fruitless search became exhausted, as indeed were we. However, we pressed on without him, showing shepherds the bird's picture in a book, disbursing *escudos* to the most unlikely people, some of whom were not difficult to persuade that they knew a man who had a cousin whose wife had seen a white bird with some black on it. As a result, we travelled many miles to look at magpies, a fatuous and discouraging exercise from which we dared not desist just in case....

34

Page 35 Elusive and difficult, this female Common Crane was
photographed at its nest on a Norwegian bog

Page 36 (*above*) 'May breed in Portugal' was the usual statement of the distribution of the Black-winged Kite in Europe. Then Derrick England sought it out, found it and photographed it; (*below*) the strange, cave-dwelling Oilbird was an obvious project for Derrick England when he cast his net wider than Europe

From one Magpie to the Next

And then one day, miles from anywhere in quite hopeless country, because the trees were no more than bushes, and very few of them at that, we were so dispirited and exhausted that we called a halt. We just could not spend the rest of our lives tramping in the scorching heat from one magpie's nest to another, even though several of them did contain young spotted cuckoos. And so, with many regretful gestures and a final bestowal of largess, we tried to make it plain to our farm-labourer guide that this was the finish—we could not take any more. 'Just one more—not more than a kilometre (this usually meant several miles)—a different nest.' 'No—not even one more'; but he looked so disappointed that of course we allowed him to take us to the most unlikely place yet: a small thickset prickly cork-oak bush with, just out of reach, what might have once been a rather flimsy jay's nest. No bird was on it, none had been seen to fly away as we approached, and it certainly was not worth getting torn and scratched climbing into the bush to look inside.

Success

At some time or other most people have had the feeling of being watched and I had it then. Sitting disconsolately beside that bush, considering how I should be greeted by the Chief Editor of *British Birds* who was shortly joining us to see what progress we had made, I was quite sure that an antagonistic eye was on me. And there on the top of a tree a couple of hundred yards away sat a white bird with black shoulders, with an air of unwelcoming resignation. I was up to that nest without pausing to think of the scratches, to find the clutch of warm kestrel-like eggs which were, so far as we knew, only the fourth to be recorded in Europe. But away, as quickly as we could, to watch her safely back, and then to base to discuss plans.

Were we justified in putting at risk so rare a bird (in Europe) by trying to photograph it at the nest? The word of eight British and (later) two Portuguese ornithologists was sufficient for record purposes. A decision had to be taken as to whether, having been found and the breeding proved, the birds should be left alone. There was little doubt that photographs were highly desirable even as records if they could be obtained without disturbance, but we had no means of assessing the reaction of the species—nor of these particular individuals—to a hide. Was their very rarity in Europe perhaps the result of an over-sensitivity to interference by man?

Testing Time

It went without saying that if we did try we must be more careful than ever before and so eventually we decided to test the birds' willingness to accept some form of alteration to the landscape at a considerable distance.

Although the nest was only 10 feet up, some form of trestle or pylon was necessary on which to mount camera and photographer high enough to look slightly downwards on to it. An ordinary 'pylon'—four poles or metal scaffolding firmly planted in the ground, with cross bracings and a platform on top—was out of the question on the score of bulk, quite apart from the difficulty of a gradual approach and the time the bird would be kept away during erection. I gave my party full marks for accepting without question, in my hearing at least, my suggestion of a tripod of three poles, lashed together a third of their length from the top, so that a triangular 'crotch' was formed into which the photographer could wedge himself with a cloth cover around him supported by the tops of the poles. The advantages of this apparently primitive arrangement were (*a*) it could be erected at a distance without the bird even being driven from the nest; (*b*) the bird's first awareness of it would be as bare poles; (*c*) it could be moved nearer quickly and easily; (*d*) if the slightest doubt arose it could be removed almost instantly; and (*e*) it required the minimum of timber, a consideration in view of the rough track which the transporting vehicle would have to traverse. The hide material was to be introduced as the tripod approached the nest, first as a wrap around one of the poles, later as a gradually spreading small tent. The rate of approach was to be determined by the reaction of the birds.

Accommodating Bird

In the event, all these precautions, although they were never regretted, were unnecessary. Many a barn-door fowl has been less approachable than these black-winged kites, and the first photographer to have a session in the hide (at a distance of 8 feet) had the bird incubating before him in minutes.

Not all birds are so accommodating as to build their nest 10 feet up in a bush on dry ground only a few hundred yards from a track, as these did. The preliminary homework required was long-winded and frustrating; the location of the birds and their nest was time-consuming and quite arduous; but the actual hide-building and photography, although they had to be done very carefully indeed because of the bird's rarity in Europe, were easy enough.

The Crane

The crane was a very different proposition. The location of

39

a breeding area was done for us in advance by a friend, who inspired us to attempt the job and who also found a nest for us in each of our first two attempts. The first of these was successful in that a pair of cranes accepted a hide, but my photographs—although they were subsequently published—were so far below what I wanted that I did not count the crane as 'done'. The following year another pair also accepted a hide, but a hooded crow sucked the eggs before my eyes and the eyes of the crane. The latter did nothing whatever to drive off the crow. I dared do nothing, because anything I did would also have driven off the crane, for good.

Following this we tried two years running in Sweden, where most cranes nest in marshy spots deep in vast forests. Here again we found nests, but hide-building was so slow, because of very difficult terrain and distance from transport, that the eggs hatched before we were able to start to photograph. In on casee there was a newly hatched chick still in the nest when I went into the hide, but it was called away by its parents without them approaching near enough for their photograph to be taken.

Back to Norway

Next we tried Denmark but, though we located the birds, we found that they were so rare there that attempts at photography would have been quite unjustified. So back to Norway where, on my seventh visit to Scandinavia for the purpose, the crane was successfully photographed.

The three main obstacles to be overcome in photographing a crane at the nest (having first located the approximate breeding area) are, first, to locate a nest; second, to find one which is accessible to man—more than half those I have seen were on such wet situations, surrounded by floodwater or bog which would neither support a man's weight nor float a boat, that they were quite unapproachable except by helicopter—third, to build a hide acceptable to the birds and to move it gradually closer (perhaps only a few feet each day) until it is in position for photography, *in the limited time between finding the nest and the hatching cf the eggs*. For, as mentioned above, the young leave the nest almost at once, and then the attempt at photography must wait until next year. The object of the exercise is thus 'to beat the hatch'. For still photography of this species the optimum distance from hide to nest is not more than 30 feet, but a satisfactory ciné film may be made from a much greater distance. One of the very best films of cranes at the nest was made from an almost unbelievable distance because the only suitable nest was in a reserve, and no permit to enter had been obtained. It was possible to overlook the nest, which fortunately was not very far from the boundary, from some high ground outside on which the hide was built. It was so far away that the birds took no notice of it!

Frozen Marshes

We, however, having found a nest which it seemed could be reached, if with difficulty, on foot, aimed at getting our hide to a distance of 30 feet, which at first sight seemed impossible because the nest was right out in the middle of a large frozen marsh, with not even a bush to break the landscape. The birds were used to complete nothingness around them. Our first step, therefore, was to 'plant' a small, 6 feet tall, birch tree about 100 feet from the nest. Even this worried the birds for a while, as we could see from a vantage-point halfway up the adjacent hill, but they soon accepted it. Next day, we added a couple more small trees to form a loose 'bush', taking care that the birds could see right through it so that their suspicions were not unduly aroused.

During the next few days we added more trees, gradually moving the whole mass nearer to the nest; it sounds easy, but it was quite a labour, since each little birch tree had to be cut down with a primitive saw, dragged out across the marsh, and set in a hole made in the ice with a crowbar in order to keep it upright. All this had to be done against the clock, for fear of keeping the birds away long enough for the eggs to become chilled in the bitter wind.

Heart in Mouth

The day came when, at 40 feet, we thickened up the bush, hollowed it out, put a small hiding-tent inside and retired with our hearts in our mouths. The cranes circled round overhead for some time, eventually landing a few hundred feet from the nest and breaking into their fantastic display, leaping high in the air, throwing their heads over their backs and trumpeting their wild clarion call. When this stopped they began to preen themselves, giving the appearance of having no interest in the nest whatever. Soon they started to work towards the nest, feeding (probably false-feeding) as they went and eventually, while one slowly moved off, the other was standing within a few feet. In a moment or two she stood right over the eggs, drew herself to her full height to have a good look around and then, with much shuffling and to our great joy, settled on her clutch.

Lens Hiding

Before moving the hide closer, I had one session at 40 feet, to test the birds' reaction to a lens, which we hid as carefully as we could, keeping it well within the hide, and to ensure, so far as possible, that some photographs were obtained even though from too far away. Although obviously wary, the birds behaved well, but I hardly dared to breathe and during a seven-hour session my sandwiches remained unopened because I feared that the crackle of paper would prove fatal.

Next day we moved up to 30 feet, but now we were beset by another trouble: the ice was thawing. A comparatively easy walk to the hide became a splashing, stumbling, wet-making adventure, while the environs of the hide, where we had worked to erect it, turned into a quagmire which might become bottomless as the thaw proceeded. A day in the hide meant, within minutes, Wellingtons full of ice-cold water and a camp-stool which all-too-quickly sank until one's pants were a wet compress. But the birds were behaving magnificently, either male or female being on the nest nearly all the time. The first time the male visited me he walked round the hide and came right up and peered into the lens. My lungs nearly burst.

Each member of the party had a turn in the hide, but we only just won the race because a youngster could be heard, from the hide, calling through a hole in a chipping egg.

Siberian White Crane

The survival of several of the fifteen species of cranes in the world is endangered, chiefly because of the gradual but inexorable decrease in the amount of wild open country which they need both for nesting and for wintering. One of the largest of these is the Siberian white crane, a large white bird with bare red skin on its face; a bird whose plumage appears to be white all over until it spreads its wings to fly, when black primaries can be seen.

Like the common crane it breeds in the north and moves south for the winter. Its nesting areas are so remote that it is only in one or two places in winter that it is likely to be seen.

43

One of these in the north of India is well known—perhaps too well known for the welfare of the birds—and some years ago I set off for Delhi as a jumping-off point to reach the unexpectedly small area of floodwater about 150 miles away at Bharatpur where a number of these magnificent birds may usually be seen at the appropriate time of year. However, I was too late: they had all left on their long and dangerous journey northwards, and so my visit could be little more than a reconnaissance.

It is no secret that, at this particular place, a few of the wintering cranes arrive about mid-November but the main body—alas getting fewer as man arrogantly and thoughtlessly makes life ever more untenable for wildlife—do not settle in until later. So, after much correspondence of the usual rather abortive type, we reserved seats on a Delhi-bound plane for early February. Apart from sticky heat and mixed food we did not anticipate any particular discomforts or difficulties. We knew that we could not expect exhibition-standard photographs because this was to be shooting-from-the-shoulder rather than hide-near-the-nest photography. Some years previously the area had wisely been designated a sanctuary—largely, I think, as a result of the efforts of Salim Ali—and we already had permission to stay there and to photograph the cranes.

Four Wasted Days

New Delhi Airport, however, is not at the best of times the most invigorating place, and at 1.30 am after a tiring plane journey it is not at its best, especially when one is greeted with the flat statement 'No cameras, no films' by the customs officer. Without the efforts of two representatives of the Indian Department of Tourism, we never should have set foot on

Indian soil; as it was, the best they could do was to get us through, while all our cameras and films were seized by the customs officials. To cut a long depressing story short, it took me four wasted days of argument at offices in different parts of the city to get them back again. The most helpful tourist department told us that they and the customs people wage a kind of Hundred Years War (although it seems doubtful whether 100 years will see the end of it); one wants to encourage tourists, the other seems bent on making things intolerable for them. (They are not alone; I could mention a bird-photographers' paradise where 50 per cent duty has to be paid on films taken into the country by tourists, and the officials decide what was the cost of the films on which they will levy their 50 per cent.)

A Gentleman from Poonah

It was while wasting four days at a pleasant hotel in Delhi that we received the most depressing news of all. One of the party, glancing through a newspaper, came across a letter from a gentleman from Poonah (or somewhere), saying that he had recently visited the sanctuary where we proposed to go and, in his forty years' experience, this was the first year in which no white cranes had turned up for the winter. (Incidentally, they were not recorded forty years ago.) Fortunately for us this gentleman must have suffered from blindness; when we eventually arrived a few days later, there were the cranes. An advance guard had turned up as usual in November and the rest around Christmas. It was worrying however that, so far as we could see, there were only three juveniles among the flock of eighty-three, a proportion which, we could not help feeling, did not augur well for the continuance of the species.

We arrived in the late afternoon, with just time to see that they really were there, and were most impressed by their approachability; it looked as though we should even be able to photograph them from the road. So, since we particularly wanted a film of them, next morning we put our ciné man in first. He exposed thousands of feet of film, only to find when they had been processed that, at the early age of forty, he had Parkinsonism, or so the camera-shake made it appear. The other two of us strongly suspected the Delhi night-clubs. I went to bed full of optimism for the morrow: I might even get close enough to avoid the need for my 400mm lens.

Pandemonium

It must have been soon after midnight when I was awakened by an indescribable pandemonium. Every crane, goose and other wildfowl was screaming in wild alarm—it must be a nightmare. But it wasn't. When at last dawn broke after one of the most ghastly nights I can remember we learnt the cause: some young ornithologists from Bombay had come over on a ringing expedition. Their methods were, to say the least, exciting. A long net had been stretched across the water where the birds were wont to spend the night. At a given signal a number of men (apparently of a lower caste than the gentlemen waiting in comfort on the bank to receive the fruits of their labours) waded in inky darkness through the water, driving in front of them a vast assortment of fowls, ranging from purple gallinules and geese to cranes of the endangered species which were the primary reason for the creation of the sanctuary. Their catch was crammed into outsize laundry-baskets and taken ashore. (We found some of these ringed birds dead or maimed next day.)

A few nights like this put paid to my hope of an easy

approach and it seemed as though the cranes were now so wary that a telescope view was all one could hope for. Even the usually very easy sarus cranes now kept their distance. But I was forgetting Hookum Singh. (I do not know how to spell his name, but then neither does he.) Without him the sanctuary would be nothing; his knowledge, helpfulness, willingness and resource are beyond belief. I was so pleased when a huge smile spread right across his face on my arrival— he remembered me from the time before. He wasn't going to be beaten just because the cranes had been frightened. Briefly our plan was this: in a little boat we erected one of the small nylon hides without which I go nowhere. With me in the hide and him in the back like an outboard motor we set off, before it was light, towards the area where a party of cranes usually spent the night. As it began to get light and we could just see vague white shapes in the distance, Hookum Singh climbed over the transom into the water: the nearer we got the lower he sank. He could not see, of course, but I guided him by signals quietly tapped out—right, left, on, slowly, stop. Very slowly and cautiously we approached, freezing whenever the cranes gave the slightest sign of restlessness, and so—even though I did need to use my 'Big Bertha', and my hands, palsied with excitement, were not holding the camera really steady—we did not have to come home with no photograph at all.

South and east of Eden

John Gooders

There was a time when birds were divided into two classes—British birds and foreigners. That such divisions are less obvious today is not only to be welcomed but is easily explained. Travel, the boom industry of the middle part of this century, is so freely available that not only have the Blackpool and Southend holiday-makers made the Costa Brava very much their own, but bird-watchers have joined in to help Europeanise our pursuits. So much are we Europeans that it is now a rare occurrence for a book purely about British birds to be published. We think in European terms and think of European birds.

The Unavailable Palaearctic

That Europe is itself a false concept zoogeographically only slowly dawned on us. Gradually the emphasis turned to the Western Palaearctic, an area that includes not only Europe but also the vast lands of North Africa, Turkey and the Soviet Union eastwards to the Urals. The concept of this region is at least sensible, coinciding with almost half of a zoogeographic region. But travel does not end at Casablanca, Cairo, Ankara or Sverdlovsk. The trouble is that much of the remainder of the Palaearctic is buried behind Soviet and Chinese frontiers, where ornithological explorations by westerners are not exactly encouraged. If things had been otherwise the travelling bird-watcher would have pushed on eastwards from Finnish Lapland in pursuit of the great breeding grounds of waders on the marshes of the Petchora and other rivers, as our ornitho-forebears did before the Revolution. That we find Terek Sandpiper and Blyth's Reed Warbler so appealing is no doubt in part due to the limited number of birds that sneak across the frontier into Finland. Thus a totally Palearctic bird-watcher is almost an impossibility at present.

Paradise

Outside the Western Palaearctic, British bird-watchers have had a natural tendency to head southwards across the Sahara with our migrant warblers, waders and hirundines; and south-eastwards along the southern fringe of the Palearctic region. This migration, built up on the back of cheap airfares and new motorable roads, has apparently been little checked by the astronomical inflation in the price of fuel. Thus, at a time when the British bird-watcher is changing from a European to a citizen of the whole avian world, it is perhaps not inappropriate to write of the paradises that can be found in these two major directions.

Roger Peterson, in his introduction to my book on *Wildlife Paradises*, says, 'Some years ago I made the pronouncement that the Flamingoes of Lake Nakuru presented the greatest bird spectacle on earth. I still hold to that opinion. . . .' The great paradise of Nakuru is top of my list too, along with another comparatively small area tucked away south of Delhi in India to which I was introduced by Derrick England, who writes of his experiences there in pursuit of the graceful and

49

rare Siberian White Crane. For me, the Kaledeo Ghana Reserve at Bharatpur is a sight only to be compared with the Flamingoes of Nakuru. In some ways it is an even more magnificent place.

Pink Masses

My first sight of Lake Nakuru was on one October evening in 1973. The light was poor and anyone in their right senses would not have bothered—but this was Nakuru and I do not know many bird-watchers capable of keeping a level head in such circumstances. Out on the lake, over a hundred yards away across the mud, walked a long string of Flamingoes. Not a very impressive sight as such. But away to the north a vast pink mass blotted out part of the lake shore. There were White Pelicans and White-breasted Cormorants nesting in the trees. A Darter flew in and a party of Black Terns skimmed gracefully by. Almost suddenly the dull light disappeared and I was left wondering whether this was really the greatest bird spot on earth, or whether the gradual drying-out process had already taken its toll.

Nakuru lies in the great African Rift Valley, no more than a morning's drive from Nairobi. Like most of the Rift Valley lakes it has no outlet and the action of evaporation has made it highly saline. Here, among its shallows, up to two million Lesser Flamingoes resort to feed along with smaller numbers of Greater Flamingoes. Just a few years ago these pink frivolities had Nakuru to themselves save for a scattering of Palearctic waders and terns, and a few herons, storks and ibises. But then someone had the bright(?) idea of introducing Tilapia, the fast-growing African fish, and before you could say 'Guinness' the lake was alive with White Pelicans.

Panic at Nakuru

The morning following our arrival we were back bright and early, though not early enough to get those fabulous yellow photographs that are obtainable just as the light begins to stream over the surrounding hills. Apart from being brighter the scene was as before: long lines of Flamingoes several hundred yards away over the drying-out shoreline. Now I almost panicked, and for an hour (actually it was ten minutes) or so I tore round all the tracks searching for masses of birds within camera range.

We crossed a freshwater channel in the north and took a track that seemed to lead toward the lake. At the end we discovered a wood-and-reed hide overlooking the mouth of the tiny rivulet and there we stayed for the rest of the morning.

Within 25 yards was a huge concentration of feeding and bathing Flamingoes and as we trained our cameras on the mass we realised why so many photographs of this tremendous spectacle have been taken, but also why so few have managed to capture it properly. Across the viewfinder I could see a band of pink separating two bands of differing blues. A larger and more powerful lens made no difference and only shortened the depth of focus. All the while the adrenalin was flowing and I had no way of working off the feeling of frustration. I sat back and thought of all of the great pictures I had seen of this place. What had they got? What was the missing ingredient in the scene before my camera? I could not rustle up a storm to add drama. I could not make the birds fly.

Other Birds

Of course the one thing I had forgotten was patience, the ability to sit down and wait for it to happen. So after a few shots, just in case the hundreds of thousands of birds suddenly decided that Lake Elementitia or Lake Harrington would be a better bet today and flew off *en masse*, I settled down to watch and enjoy myself. Only then did I notice the marsh terns bathing in the fresh water a few yards before my eyes. Dive and shake in the air seemed to be the routine. A party of Yellow-billed Storks rested on their haunches to the left, while on the muddy shore to the right a few Curlew Sandpipers tripped alongside a nice flock of Little Stints. Hottentot Teal and Red-billed Duck found a little open water for themselves among the pink, and suddenly a little more as a Marabou Stork glided low over the heads of the Flamingoes sending them pattering, long-legged, over the water. A Black-winged Stilt wandered upstream and into range.

Pink Spectacular

Then slowly the Flamingoes began to fly in. Twenty or thirty at a time they came from the left, to drop down among the already gathered mass. Flock after flock arrived until right in front of us, and no more than 25 yards away, there was a mass in either direction that must have been at least a hundred yards deep. Now the viewfinder was covered with pink and I started taking photographs in earnest. Mass shots, individual shots, taking-off shots, flight shots, 'arty-type' shots, stomping shots in which the birds bunch even closer together and strut in unison. By the end of the day I had exposed nearly 400 shots of Flamingoes. Surely among that lot there must be a couple of good ones?

Lake Nakuru is by no means a one-species paradise, but its birds are nothing special without the Flamingo spectacular. In one corner we found a Black Heron busily forming an umbrella of his wings over his head to aid his hunting. There

Page 53 Wider horizons pose problems in finding birds that locals
may be able to help with, aided by the familiar field guide

Page 54 (*above*) Lesser Flamingoes on the stomp at Lake Nakuru, arguably the greatest bird sight on earth; (*below*) Greater Flamingoes patter away over the surface of Lake Nakuru, an always moving wildlife spectacular

were Pink-backed Pelicans in the trees, and a vast concourse of White Pelicans gathered in fishing parties dipping their opened bills in unison as a fish trap. Later they too came in to bathe before us. A Crowned Hawk-eagle caught our attention, and a Yellow-throated Longclaw (with the Meadowlarks of North America the usual textbook example of convergent evolution) sought its prey among the grass.

No Place for Listing

No doubt a huge list of species could be amassed at Nakuru and its surrounding grasslands and woods, but those who just do this must lack something in their soul. The spectacle of the greatest bird show on earth is no backdrop for a hard day's ticking. To visit Nakuru is to seek an experience and that is a bit more than a new bird for the life list—even a hundred new birds come to that. I had six new birds on my first day at Nakuru but I cannot say that any of them made much impression on me. Perhaps one day I shall find them somewhere else and enjoy them for their own sake.

By good fortune I was to run into John Williams, doyen of African ornithologists, in the heat of the afternoon. We performed a passable rendering of the 'Dr Livingstone I presume' routine and exchanged gossip about a strange 'stint-peep' that had haunted the lake for a few days. John was escorting an American couple who, as luck would have it, I had last met in the jungles of Nepal. If that doesn't sound like place-name dropping I don't know what does, but it's a strangely small world once you start moving from paradise to paradise in search of birds.

Throughout Kenya, and even in a thriving township like Nakuru, there is a sense of space and time. There are crowds, people hanging about and selling their wares, boys ready to mend punctures, but there is still plenty of space. In India there are people everywhere, hundreds of millions of bodies. Space is hard to find and when you think you've found it then the cattle arrive. The Kaledeo Ghana Sanctuary at Bharatpur is a tiny speck, yet even here cattle and buffalo have grazing rights that are tearing the landscape apart. There are more cattle than are permitted and they graze for longer hours than stipulated. But it is difficult with an overstrained economy like India's to see what government can do.

A Good Day's Slaughter

Where Nakuru is a spectacle, the marshes at Bharatpur are more or less a seething mass of birds, but of an incredible variety of species. Though inter-connected by waterways Bharatpur consists of a series of quite large lagoons separated by embankments lined with trees, along which one can drive or walk. Such a system makes for ideal bird-watching. Of course it was not designed so. The Sanctuary was formerly the hunting reserve of the Maharajah of Bharatpur, a place where visiting dignitaries could indulge themselves in shooting-up the vast concourse of migrants that poured out of the Eastern Palearctic. On a single day before the last war, Lord Linlithgow, at the time Viceroy and representative of Britain, managed to bag over 4,000 birds with the help of a few friends. That such a small area could survive such onslaught is testimony to the immense richness of birds to be found there and to the ability of the Indian authorities who turned it into a reserve.

On my first visit the lagoons were lit by the low light of a rising sun. Conditions were perfect and birds stood out against the pastel reds and pinks of aquatic vegetation. Painted Storks stood among the tree-tops in forlorn little groups, nearly fledged youngsters left behind by the mass exodus at the end of the breeding season. Little Cormorants and Indian Darters spread their wings and almost every 'empty' tree proved to contain an eagle keeping the waterbirds away. Spotted and Lesser Spotted, Steppe and Crested Serpent Eagles were everywhere, and there were Grey-headed Fishing Eagles, White-eyed Buzzards and the magnificent Pallas's Fishing Eagle as well.

The White Crane

But inevitably one's eyes were drawn to the pools where, among the herons and ibises, Siberian White Cranes stepped delicately in small family groups. These all-white cranes, marked only with black wing tips and bare red faces, breed in two or three remote areas of eastern Siberia and migrate southwards to winter at Bharatpur, a few spots in Afghanistan and in the Middle East and perhaps China. It is by any standards a rare bird and one that is in immense danger of disappearing altogether. It is also a very fine bird and one which we should spare no efforts to save. Indeed if half the money spent on protecting Avocets, geese and other odds and ends in this country were devoted to the White Cranes, their survival need not be viewed with such pessimism.

The Wealth of Bharatpur

While the Crane is the star of the Bharatpur show, it does not dominate the spectacle. I saw about fifty birds in February during three days. Much more numerous is the huge Sarus Crane which stalks the shallows and dances its courtship rituals on almost every pool. Cattle Egrets perch on the buffalo. Pond Herons, or Paddybirds, fly away on a flash of

57

white wings. The Great White Egret, the same bird that is so rare through Europe, is common and plentiful, while the Little Egret is, in comparison, scarce. Unfortunately named Intermediate Egrets (Plumed Egrets in Australia—a much nicer name) are everywhere, and Spoonbills gather in small parties at specially favoured feeding grounds. White and Black Ibises can be found and every lagoon holds hordes of duck—familiar Pintail, Shoveler, Teal, Wigeon, Garganey, Gadwall, Tufted Duck and Pochard, along with less familiar Red-crested Pochard, Ferruginous Duck and Ruddy Shelduck (called Brahminy Duck here). Spot-billed Duck are new, as are the delightful Cotton Teal or Indian Pygmy Geese. Moorhens offer a taste of home, but there are White-breasted Waterhens, Ruddy Crakes, Purple Gallinules and Pheasant-tailed and Bronze-winged Jacanas as well. Geese honk noisily overhead, Siberian Greylags and Bar-headed Geese that nest only in Tibet and fly over the great Himalayas to winter in northern India. Beautiful birds that are as numerous here as anywhere in the world.

Strange Mixture

This strange mixture of the familiar and unfamiliar is part of the appeal of going eastwards rather than southwards from Europe. Bharatpur is only just outside the Palearctic boundary which runs the length of the Himalayan chain to the north. The result is a curious mixture of influences which the collection of waders shows to advantage. Wood Sandpiper from Europe, Lesser Golden Plover from America and adjacent Siberia and Red-wattled Lapwing which breeds in India can all be found. And the passerines too come from widely differing areas: Woodchat Shrike, Tailorbird, Bluethroat and Blyth's Reed Warbler. The latter posed a problem in identi-

58

fication that I'm not sure now that I have solved satisfactorily.

Like Nakuru, Bharatpur is not only a reserve for birds. Sambar, the large Indian deer, were seen crossing a shallow lagoon to doze quietly on one of the artificial islands. And Blackbuck, beautiful but elusive, were found in an open area among the parkland that surrounds the marsh. Chital were found here too. But all of these animals are present in tiny numbers, apparently doomed by the destruction and over-grazing of the cattle herds.

Imminent Destruction

Bharatpur, like Nakuru, is an outstandingly beautiful place, a fine wildlife paradise, and perhaps the greatest bird sanctuary in all Asia. But whereas tourists are the bane of one's life in Africa, in India it is ordinary working people. They are colourful and friendly, but their very existence threatens to destroy this place.

Within a few days of leaving Bharatpur I was to visit Calcutta, a city not much more than 300 years old in which urban civilisation has virtually broken down. Two million people live on the streets, sheltering from the elements in cardboard cabins. Even more live in wretched tenements where the best-housed creature is the landlord's buffalo. Garbage piles up in the streets, cracked water-mains create pools around the traffic islands, sewage flows openly along the gutters and 10,000 people bed down on the third largest bridge in the world. Faced with such problems how can the Indians be expected to save their own wildlife? Surely we in the west can find enough resources to save tiny Bharatpur, the Siberian White Crane and perhaps even the tiger?

In visiting Nakuru and Bharatpur I fulfilled two major ambitions. But I hear that the Chinchas in Peru may surpass both—islands where up to 20 million seabirds gather to breed. Then there are the Galapagos, Darwin's enchanted isles, where birds await their portraiture with the patience of well-disciplined models. And what of the Snow Geese migrations along the flyways of the United States? Or the penguin rookeries of Antarctica? There are so many spectacles to choose from, but if you choose Nakuru or Bharatpur you will not be disappointed.

The whitethroat story

Kenneth Williamson

Selborne, May 21, 1770

The severity and turbulence of last month so interrupted the regular process of summer migration that some of the birds do but just begin to show themselves, and others are apparently thinner than usual; as the whitethroat, the blackcap, the redstart, the flycatcher. I well remember that after the very severe spring in the year 1739–40, summer birds of passage were very scarce. They come probably hither with a southeast wind, or when it blows between those points; but in that unfavourable year the winds blowed the whole spring and summer through from the opposite quarters.

Letter VI to the Honourable Daines Barrington

In ornithological history one cannot go much further back than the Rev Gilbert White, parish priest of Selborne in Hampshire—and how interesting it is that this observant man noted a connection between cold, inclement springs and the scarcity of some of our familiar summer visitors. Meteorology was then just emerging as a science; climatology was yet unborn. Our present knowledge of both tempts us to say that the cold springs of 1740 and 1770 (and perhaps others around those times) were due to blocking anticyclones above Scandinavia and a weak circulation over the Atlantic. Further, that this situation may well have been associated with a weakening of the monsoon winds off the coast of West Africa, and a corresponding rainfall deficiency in the winter quarters of these birds.

Ups and Downs of Common Birds

Two hundred years after Gilbert White noted cause and effect we think we have the explanation, as a result of inquiring into why the Whitethroat population crashed sensationally in 1969. In the nature of things, since climate is not static, there must have been longer or shorter periods when Whitethroat, Redstart, Whinchat, Wheatear and others of our common summer visitors were relatively scarce by comparison with their best years; but no writer seems to have noticed it. Indeed, it is difficult to be sure of the ups and downs of a common bird, since one is loath to put much confidence in subjective impressions. Today, in Britain, we have a proven method of measuring the annual fluctuations in population levels of many birds, residents and summer visitors, because our countryside is blessed with a sufficiency of amateur naturalists—modern Gilbert Whites—to gather the data required.

This is performed through the Common Birds Census of the British Trust for Ornithology, now at the end of its twelfth year. Over 200 observers take part, mapping the birds' territories, largely by plotting the positions of singing males, on the same sample plot on regular visits throughout each breeding season. The census covers about 20,000 acres and investigates all kinds of habitat, but primarily farmland and woodland. Analysis and summation of the results produce species totals which are comparable one year with the next, thus giving an 'annual index' of abundance.

Surveillance Operation

The Common Birds Census is therefore an important surveillance operation, sensitive enough to show the effects of major habitat changes in particular areas, and climatic effects on the national scale. This became obvious quite early on when, after the severe winter of 1962–3, many resident species declined, some (like the Wren and Song Thrush) drastically. It soon became clear that there were fluctuations in non-resident birds too, but until the late 1960s these appeared to follow a pattern of gradual increase, or movement either side of a mean value.

Then, between 1968 and 1969, there was a marked decline in numbers of several summer visitors, chiefly the White-throat, whose population-level fell dramatically by 77 per cent, but also Sedge and Garden Warblers, Sand Martin, Spotted Flycatcher and Yellow Wagtail. It was clear that whatever had happened to these birds had not happened in Britain, since their population levels in 1968 had been high. For the Whitethroat, 1968 was better than any previous year; many moved into woodland to breed, though this is primarily a bird of hedgerows and scrub. My own woodland plot, which had not previously had breeding Whitethroats, had no fewer than seven singing males that year. Moreover, judging by the numbers trapped and ringed at the bird observatories during autumn migration, it was a highly productive breeding season with a bumper crop of young birds surviving to emigrate.

Two Possibilities

There seemed to be two possibilities. Either the White-throats had sustained heavy losses during the autumn journey south or their return movement in spring 1969; or they had suffered badly in their winter quarters in West Africa. Both migrations are protracted, and to suffer casualties on the scale indicated by the 1969 'annual index', vast numbers must have

63

encountered sudden freak storms over a wide area, or adverse weather during a very long period. The meteorological records gave no evidence that either phenomenon had occurred. On most days, in both seasons, the weather appeared to be favourable.

Possibly some other factor, perhaps undue exposure to toxic chemicals, had been involved. The autumn of 1968 had witnessed an invasion of desert locusts on an unusually large scale in north-west Africa, and the swarms had been sprayed to protect citrus and other crops. Most of the spraying in Morocco was in the Sous Valley, and was done in November and December, by which time the majority of the White-throats should have reached their winter quarters farther south, beyond the Sahara Desert. The chemical used, DDVP (dichlorovos), has a high toxicity against locusts, but is not persistent, so would not endanger returning passage birds in spring. Smaller areas in Mauritania and Mali, closer to their winter home, were sprayed with low-dosage rates of dieldrin. All in all, there seems to be every justification for the remark of one anti-locust research worker that the affected areas were small and widely scattered, 'like cricket pitches in an English county'.

Anti-Locust Spraying

As with the weather during migration, there was nothing in the anti-locust warfare consistent with so great a diminution of Whitethroats. Indeed, a far greater quantity of insecticide, in particular the highly toxic and persistent dieldrin, had been used over a much wider area during locust control a decade before. In 1959 in Morocco alone some 8,000 square kilometres were sprayed, compared with 600 square kilometres in 1968, apparently without damage to the birds.

64

Two new factors entered the situation in the breeding seasons after 1969. Firstly, reports from the Continent showed that it was not only British Whitethroats which had dramatically declined. It was known by 1972 that all was not well with the Swedish stock; in this case too toxic chemicals, picked up not in Africa but when crossing Europe in spring, fell under suspicion; but Berthild Persson of Lund University showed that the amounts concerned did not impair fertility and could not have caused lasting harm.

Ringing Totals Down

In 1973 P. Berthold drew together a number of scattered observations which pointed to a general decline of the species in western Europe, perhaps as far to the east as Vienna. He considered that applications of pesticides in Africa had played the major role. He reported a fall of 87 per cent in migrants passing through Heligoland Bird Observatory off the North Sea coast—a bumper total of 614 ringed in 1968 was followed by a lowest-ever catch of 77 the following spring. Near Radolfzell on Lake Constance in south-west Germany the decline between 1968 and 1972 was 88 per cent. Ringing totals were substantially down at places as far apart as Hesselø in Denmark and the Camargue in southern France. There were tell-tale ringing statistics now available in Britain too— only 1,797 free-flying birds trapped in 1969 compared with 10,205 in the previous year, and only 100 nestlings marked as against 800 in 1968. In that year the BTO's Nest Record Scheme received 326 completed cards for Whitethroat nests, but only 45 came to hand in 1969.

Secondly, the Whitethroat has failed signally to show any sign of recovery, if one excepts a very slight upward movement (later reversed) in 1970–1. A number of bird-watchers have told me they saw more Whitethroats about in 1974, but even if this is so the improvement is slight. In June 1965 I took a bird-census team to Gibraltar Point Nature Reserve in Lincolnshire, where we mapped 89 territories in the sea-buckthorn of the dune ridges and salt-marsh margins, a density of one pair to the acre. A repeat census by Robert Morgan in 1974 gave barely a quarter of this total, in what is manifestly a well-favoured habitat.

Lack of Recovery

Such is the resilience of most birds that whatever factors depressed the Whitethroat population in the first place must still be operating to keep its numbers in check. We have quantitative data on the relatively rapid recovery of species as diverse as the Heron (the object of a BTO investigation over the past 46 years) and the Wren. Their numbers tumble after severe winters like 1948–9 and 1962–3, but build up to the previous level within three or four years. The continued scarcity of Whitethroats argues strongly against such causes as freak weather during migration, and exposure to toxic chemicals, since neither is likely to be repeated on a large enough scale year after year. A climatic change which has not yet been reversed, and is extensive and powerful enough to have affected the species' winter ecology, seems to be the only plausible explanation.

The world is now well aware that a change of the necessary magnitude did occur, quite suddenly, in 1968. The monsoon winds off the west African coast were weaker than usual, and the rains which normally fall between June and October failed to penetrate to the semi-arid steppe country bordering the southern edge of the Sahara Desert—the so-called Sahel Zone where the Whitethroats have their winter home. These rains

66

have always been somewhat unpredictable in their timing, location and amount: an area may have a copious fall one year and very little the next; sometimes the rain comes early, sometimes late.

From a fairly low value in 1949 precipitation over the region as a whole increased to 160 per cent of normal (ie the average value for the 30 years 1931–60) in 1950, and continued to be well above normal during the next decade. During most of the 1960s it fluctuated about the mean level until the fateful year 1968, when it plunged to 25 per cent below normal. It has remained low since, apart from a minor upsurge in 1969 when northern Sénégal, southern and central Mauritania had useful rains. It may be significant that Sedge and Garden Warblers, Redstart, Whitethroat and Yellow Wagtail all showed a slightly improved status in Britain in 1970.

The deterioration has been least marked along the coast, only 5 per cent below normal, but has grown with latitude northwards to reach an accumulated deficiency 250–300 per cent of normal since 1968 on the desert fringe between 16° and 18° N. Stations in the Sahel which formerly reported 100–150mm of rain per annum are now recording 4–6mm only, and the isohyets (lines on the map joining points of equal rainfall amounts) in Mauritania and Chad have been displaced some 200 (and locally up to 400) kilometres farther south than usual.

Vacant Niches

The Sahel Zone serves a number of west European species as winter quarters, and one reason may be that they have almost no competition for food from African species. Some, like the Willow and Garden Warblers, the Pied and Spotted Flycatchers, and some of the Nightingales, stay there for a few weeks following their arrival, and then move farther south; why is not known, but perhaps they then find a niche which some African bird has vacated. The Whitethroat remains in the Sahel Zone throughout the dry season (it is extremely scarce south of 11° N) and its environment is steadily deteriorating during that time. Despite the absence of rain between October and May, there remains enough arthropod and vegetable food to see the Whitethroats safely through the winter in a normal rainfall year. As Gerard Morel points out in a note in *Ibis* (1973), many evergreen trees and shrubs are in flower, host to various insects, when the birds arrive, and he names six species which bear berries on which the wintering warblers feed. Nevertheless, they need to be widely dispersed, and in the hottest months, February and March, the density in the scrub is usually not more than two birds per hectare.

Taking on Migration Fuel

Berries are of vital importance late in their stay, helping them to lay down sufficient fat reserves for the 2,000 miles flight across the Sahara Desert. Fry, Elgood and Ferguson-Lees, in *Ibis* (1972), report that at Malamfatori on Lake Chad, Garden Warblers put on 1gm, Whitethroats 0·6gm, and the smaller Sedge Warblers 0·2gm per day on average in late March and early April on a diet of *Lantana* berries, while the remnant flood pools have vast swarms of a green midge *Tanytarsus spadiceonotatus* on which Yellow Wagtails and Sand Martins feed. Indeed, species which normally winter well to the south of the Sahel Zone, even beyond the Equator, may rely largely on the resources of this final staging-post to give them strength for the long hop to the Mediterranean.

This is mainly conjecture for we know very little concerning the late-winter ecology of our summer migrants in Africa, but

68

it is almost certainly true in the case of aerial plankton feeders like the martins and swallows.

Famine Disorder

If the recent history of the Sahel Zone had been otherwise, the drop in Whitethroat numbers might have been gradual rather than catastrophic. There have been drought periods in this region before, yet there is no indication in the literature that Whitethroats or any other species suffered badly. However, the last big rainfall deficiency coincided with the First World War, when ornithologists were constrained to think of things other than birds.

During the 1950s the rainfall generally was well above average, and a number of West African states which had newly acquired their independence took this opportunity to settle the semi-arid steppe, and to encourage the native nomad tribes to rear cattle on an intensive scale to provide meat for the developing coastal towns. Compared with previous decades the interior of Sénégal, Mauritania, Mali, Upper Volta, Niger and Chad became grossly overpopulated with people and animals. The failure of the rains in the summer of 1968 and afterwards consequently created a famine situation such as this region had never known; and even the social and economic life-pattern of the nomad tribes, adjusted through many generations to the harsh alternation of drought and plenty, could not cope.

Disappearing Shrubs

In 1973 alone $3\frac{1}{2}$ million cattle died, there was a grain shortage of a million tons, and six million people faced starvation. Long before that, in order to stay alive, the herds had concentrated near the waterholes, and had eaten up the vegetation for many miles around. Faced with such over-grazing any chance of regeneration was removed, and the berry-bearing shrubs on which the wintering birds and migrants depend must have disappeared without trace from vast areas. No wonder the southwards march of the Sahara Desert is said to have exceeded 400 kilometres in some places.

Blocking Anticyclones

Climatic changes are not independent of one another. The driving-belt of earth's atmosphere is the upper westerlies, and a change in the position or strength of the troughs downstream of the main continents, and of the ridges downstream of the main oceans, has profound effects on the weather-making processes within the linked vertical circulations in the lower atmosphere. A change in wave-length in the upper westerlies in recent years has resulted in an intensification of the polar anticyclone and a weakening of the circulation over the Atlantic Ocean. A pronounced ridge or 'blocking anticyclone' over Scandinavia now keeps the Atlantic depressions at bay and brings us cold, dry north-easters, in place of the mild wet westerlies of earlier years, in late winter and spring.

These developments have had interesting repercussions on the status in Britain of some northern birds. North of the equator the rain-making processes within the vertical Hadley Cell circulation appear to have been reversed, so that precipitation is now greater in its descending branch over North Africa than in the weakened ascending one south of the Sahara. There can be little doubt that the effects are global in scope, that recent droughts in Brazil, West Africa, Ethiopia, Arabia and India are closely linked, and that compensatory changes are going on in the southern hemisphere as well. In

Page 71 (*above*) Wintering at Bharatpur, the very rare Siberian White Crane is a major attraction at the best wetland in Asia and another challenge for Derrick England's camera; (*below*) the answer to the dramatic and sudden decline in Whitethroats along our hedgerows was sought in the arid Sahel zone south of the Sahara

Page 72   Fifty thousand Wood Sandpipers regularly congregate in
the Camargue each autumn to take on fuel in the form of fat prior to
a trans-Saharan flight

our own small country, the connection between cold springs and a dearth of summer migrants, noted so long ago by Gilbert White, is very real.

Whitethroat Future

Meanwhile, what does the future hold for the Whitethroat? Dr Derek Winstanley, a student of the world's rainfall regimes, has prophesied a temporary improvement in the Sahel around 1980, but he regards this as an irregular fluctuation in a long downward trend which is part of a 200 year cycle. Not much hope for the Whitethroat there! Will it adjust to the new situation by seeking winter quarters farther south? This may take time, especially if it has to wait until some wintering Palaearctic or wandering African species retires in its turn, so leaving a vacant niche. Perhaps the most ominous point to have emerged from the Whitethroat story, thus far, is that while species are able to adapt to the more gradual, long-term changes, the dramatic short-term fluctuations superimposed upon them leave bird populations no room for manoeuvre, and can inflict a drastic change of status. Both levels of change are important in the study of population dynamics, particularly as it is not yet clear to what extent recovery from the latter is possible, and we need monitoring devices like the Common Birds Census to enable us to identify and study such developments.

Wings over the Sahara

C. Hilary Fry

It is not so very long ago that ornithologists were unable to accept some of the implications of the known fact that numerous European and Asiatic birds wintered in equatorial and southern Africa. It may have been accepted, in the absence of any but the most circumstantial and fragmentary evidences, that some large birds like Black Kites or fast fliers like Garganey might follow routes regularly taking them over corners of the Saraha. Generally most people were unable to credit that smaller birds reached their winter quarters by any route other than the verdant valley of the Nile, and to a much lesser extent the Atlantic coast and the borders of the Red Sea.

Worst Journey in the World

We are now forced to recognise that even the most fragile and vulnerable birds make broad-front crossings not only of the Sahara, the greatest and most barren desert in the world, but in the same journey of the Mediterranean, or the Red Sea together with the Arabian Desert, requiring feats of endurance and navigation that were formerly unimaginable.

This realisation has dawned so slowly partly because many aspects of migration are difficult phenomena to investigate, and it is only since the use of tracking radar as a research tool became widespread that much sound knowledge about the routes of many migrant species within Europe and North America has been gained. So far as Africa is concerned, however, it is still true that very few radar studies have been made. Working from information furnished by ships' radars in the Mediterranean, Casement in 1966 demonstrated that migrants do not restrict themselves to the 'safe' crossing at Gibraltar, and nor even do they concentrate to any important extent at such narrower crossings as between the toe of Italy, Sicily and Tunis. Instead they crisscross the Mediterranean at all points, flying unseen by all except the radar's eye by night and also by day.

Prying Eye of Radar

From a radar installation in Niger, on the southern border of the Sahara, Schaefer showed that in autumn echoes attributable to wildfowl, waders and passerines moved on a southern and south-south-westerly bearing, having crossed one of the broadest and most frightful parts of the desert. Further radar studies made in the 1970s in Sudan and Ghana confirm the view that the geography of desert, river, seas, landmass and elevation apparently makes precious little difference to the route followed by a bird, once it has fuelled and embarked upon its definitive migratory flight, until it arrives at its final destination, or a major intermediary one, whether on the autumn or the spring flights.

Distracting Natives

Another reason for the slow growth of knowledge on trans-Saharan migration is that the wealth of native bird life in

75

Africa has tended to distract attention from Palaearctic species wintering there. This is understandable enough, although it is astonishing to think, in view of what we do know now, that a little over a decade ago the data on the distribution, abundance and biology of even the commonest temperate-zone visitors to the tropics was scanty indeed.

Much of the work on bird migration between Eurasia (the Palaearctic) and sub-Saharan Africa is linked with the name of the late R. E. Moreau. From early days he was interested in the problem of bird flight over the Sahara, and its implications for their physiological performance. He gathered observations together in a series of key papers between 1961 and 1967, 'Problems of Mediterranean-Saharan migration' and 'Water birds over the Sahara'. His lifelong studies culminated in a treatise published posthumously in 1972: 'The Palaearctic-African Bird Migration Systems', which was based in large part on the field studies of many ornithologists in Africa in the 1960s. Before that, it was possible to say for many European species little more about their occurrence in Africa than that sporadic sight and skin records had established their wintering presence in one or another major region of the continent.

Breakthrough

Then in 1966 a paper on Palaearctic birds in Nigeria showed that more than 120 Palaearctic species occurred regularly there, many in great abundance. Analysis also produced the surprising result that hardly any species penetrate the rain-forest zone (Nightingales, Wood Warblers, Pied Flycatchers and Honey-Buzzards are among the few exceptions). Moreover, while a number of land-bird species do seek out the lusher woodlands bordering the equatorial rain forest, the great majority of species winter in the drier and less-promising-

76

looking types of vegetation to the north, farther from the rain forest and closer to the desert. The moist and dry savanna woodland of the southern tropics of Africa contain many fewer winter visitors than are found north of the Equator, and again this is contrary to expectation; for the time that these birds are in Africa coincides with the rains in the southern tropics but with the dry season in the north, and a drought that becomes progressively more severe towards the time in spring when the visitors fatten up for their return migration over the Sahara.

Rather few land-bird species from the temperate zone find their way into southern Africa, though the Swallow is a notable exception. A number of Palaearctic bird visitors to South Africa have even stayed on to nest there, finding ecological conditions not too dissimilar from those in their original breeding areas of the warmer parts of Europe and Asia. Bee-eaters often breed in southern Africa; less frequently, White Storks, Black Storks, House Martins and Swallows have stayed on to do so.

Wintering Waterbirds

In general, water birds are rather more widespread in their Africa have even stayed on to nest there, finding ecological conditions not too dissimilar from those in their original breeding great lakes and rivers, particularly where falling water levels expose plenty of sand and mud. White Storks are widespread within suitable wetlands within the savanna zones, and several species of herons migrate across the Sahara from natal areas in southern Europe. Ringing recoveries substantiate this assertion; otherwise it would be difficult to prove, since all of the European species of herons also breed in Africa, where moreover many of them have intratropical migrations in time with the movements of the populations from Europe.

Lake Chad

A brief account of bird life at Lake Chad will give an impression of the abundance and diversity of Palaearctic migrants in the African scene. This shallow lake, fringed by alternating beaches and papyrus beds backing on to scrub-covered sand dunes, has been a focus of migration research because it lies in the arid Sahel Zone and abuts the southern border of the Sahara. In spring it might be expected to concentrate migrants arriving from the south seeking a suitable fuelling refuge as close as possible to the desert. In the event, the great concentrations of Palaearctic birds discovered on the shores of Lake Chad exceeded all expectations. Three species, Ruff, Sand Martin and Yellow Wagtail, are to be numbered in millions. The open waters of the lake have rather few birds, and only White-winged Black Terns are at all common. But on the strand many waders feed alongside the hordes of wagtails: Ringed, Little Ringed and Kentish Plovers, Greenshank, Marsh, Green, Wood and Common Sandpipers. Interspersed are less common waterside birds, like Spoonbills and Glossy Ibis; and a few records of vagrants such as White-tailed Lapwings, Greater Sand Plovers and Caspian Plovers show how much easting some birds have to make during their return passage to the Palaearctic. Ducks are not very common on the open waters of the lake, but in sheltered pools amid reeds Garganey are found, with lesser numbers of Ferruginous Duck, Shoveler, Pintail and of course the native species.

Globe Spanners

Other common species along the shore lines are Red-throated Pipits and Wheatears. The former does not breed south of the Arctic Circle, while the latter has breeding populations in Greenland, across Europe and Asia to Kamchatka and east of the Bering Straits in Alaska, all of which winter in Africa. Thus both Red-throated Pipits and Wheatears at Lake Chad will be embarking on journeys of extraordinary magnitude. We do not yet know the precise destination in Eurasia of those Wheatears that spend the winter in the sandy wastes around Lake Chad or are spring passage migrants fattening there. But from some other localities south of the Sahara if not this one, the species will leave upon a diagonal crossing of the desert and continue over the Red Sea or Palestine area towards Transcaucasia, thereafter continuing to a destination (for the Alaskan population) no less than 11,000km from Khartoum. This is the *shortest* distance between origin and destination, calculating upon a Great Circle route. Other wintering populations of Wheatears presumably return to their breeding grounds on a more northerly heading, to western Europe; or even substantially west of north, in the case of birds repairing to Greenland. Incidentally, so distant are eastern Siberia and Alaska from central Africa that the shortest or Great Circle route passes over the top of the globe, not far from the North Pole itself. It means that *if* migrants follow a Great Circle track they can be expected to leave their Siberian breeding grounds in autumn on a heading initially *north* of west, not south of it.

Papyrus Swamps

The reed, mace and papyrus beds around the lake are full of Reed, Sedge and Great Reed Warblers, and they seem to pick an easy living in spring by feeding upon the rich insect life, despite competition by many species of native *Acrocephalus* and *Cisticola* warblers in the same habitat. A few Savi's

79

Warblers have turned up here, while a number of birds have been netted in the last few years which were formerly thought to be Africa's first records of Blyth's Reed Warblers (a north-west Russian bird that winters in India), but have now been described as a new race of African Reed Warbler, probably migrant, and almost exactly intermediate in biological characteristics between equatorial African Reed Warblers and Blyth's Reed Warbler. Sand Martins forage in enormous numbers above the reedbeds, and migrating Persian Bee-eaters hawk for dragonflies above them.

Impenetrable Thickets

A few hundred yards from the shore lines there are low sand dunes topped with impenetrable thickets of Saltbush *Salvadora*, and a great many Palaearctic species feed upon the berries of this plant and seek its shade—Redstarts, Woodchats, Wrynecks, Olivaceous Warblers, Blackcaps and Whitethroats, Lesser Whitethroats, Subalpine Warblers: the list seems endless, especially when native birds are also taken into account. Farther away from the lakeside, *Salvadora* thickets become more sparse and are replaced by light woodland of stunted thorny trees, mainly *Acacias* and *Balanites*.

Missing Migrants

Even in this rather unpromising-looking environment there are many Eurasian birds, the ubiquitous wagtails and Whitethroats, Wheatears, shrikes, Rollers and—locally, in great abundance—Turtle-doves. The last species still presents something of an enigma, although to a lesser extent than formerly; for the droves of Turtle-doves that can be seen in autumn passing over the Apollo coast or coasting in Sicily,

Cyprus or down the Nile seem to vanish into thin air on entering the Sahara. It is known that concentrations of tens of thousands are to be found in parts of Senegal and in a narrow corridor, in mature *Acacia* woodland near permanent water, from north-west Nigeria to Ethiopia, although records are still sparse in view of the millions of Turtle-doves that must occur somewhere in Africa. There are several such mystery migrants; another is the Barred Warbler, abundant in eastern Europe and Asia, wintering apparently only in east central Africa between the Equator and about 10° N, yet nowhere recorded in any abundance. In 1972 a large concentration was found in the arid, desert country around the south end of Lake Rudolf, but it is too soon to say whether a major segment of the species' populations winter there.

Routes Across the Sahara

From ringing controls, the average directions of movement of a few species between African ringing stations and Eurasian recovery areas—and hence their direction across the Sahara— are known in some detail. Swallows ringed in Kenya have been recovered in a region to the north-west of the Caspian. Red-backed Shrikes and Lesser Grey Shrikes are known, partly from ringing recoveries and partly from locality/date plotting of records, to follow a 'loop' migration, entering the tropics in autumn by crossing the eastern Sahara, and returning in spring (from southern Africa in the case of Lesser Grey Shrikes) well to the east, along the Nile or perhaps crossing the Red Sea to concentrate in the Near East. More detailed information still is available for Yellow Wagtails. Hordes of them winter all over the African savannas, and they must be among the most abundant Palaearctic visitors. They have attracted the attention of migration workers there not only on this account, but also because of the racial differences in plumage, in males, which become so well marked in the pre-nuptial moult about February/March that it is often possible to assert with some confidence, even by viewing in the field, that an individual Yellow Wagtail will return to breeding grounds in the Balkans, in Scandinavia or in central Russia. Probably over 50,000 birds of this species have now been marked in Africa, mainly in Nigeria and Kenya; the Nigerian birds have yielded over 100 controls abroad, a few in North Africa, many in Italy, and most around the Gulf of Bothnia.

Multi-racial

The various races of wagtails are not, however, segregated geographically in Africa as they are upon their nesting grounds. On the contrary, there is a considerable mixture of races in Africa; while some subspecies evidently have rather circum-scribed winter ranges (British Yellow Wagtails *Motacilla flava flavissima*, for instance, winter largely in Liberia), others range trans-continentally in winter. At Lake Chad, eleven races were recorded within three weeks on spring passage, bound for destinations from Spain to the Aral Sea.

Despite the variations in mean flight direction that these various populations make, on balance birds cross the western, central and eastern Sahara in spring on a north-north-east heading. Birds emigrating from Lake Chad would be unlikely to depart from a latitude much north of 13° N, food resources for most species then being extremely scant. Assuming they make a NNE crossing and a landfall in the nearest verdant parts of North Africa, they would have a journey of 1,500 to 2,200km. For most small passerines, allowing for the following winds in spring at 2,000 metres (a common migratory altitude across the Sahara), a flight of this distance would take 25 to 45 hours, depending upon direction, ground-speed and wind. Wagtails are one of the few species that might be able to refuel themselves at oases on the way—indeed they have been found doing so in Tripolitania (although robust individuals may well not normally break their trans-Saharan flight at all). But most species are obliged, it seems, to make this flight without rest or refuelling. Few observers have recorded migrants at desert oases or waddies, except in numbers sufficiently small to suggest that they are only the fallout, weak individuals doomed as surely as the occasional warblers or chats found by travellers crossing the central Sahara pathetically seeking the shade of a stone.

Fat for Fuel

The energetics of the prodigious feat of flying the Sahara are of much interest. Fuel for the journey is stored by all long-distance migrants as fats and oils, in depots located around and between the viscera, over the pectoral muscles and between the arms of the wishbone (furcula). Small birds deposit an amount of lipid equal to their own lean weight, that is they double their weight before migrating. This gain takes place very rapidly, in a matter of two or three weeks, so that White-throats, for instance, in fattening from 13 to 26gm, put down nearly 1gm of lipid a day. Contrary to expectation, feeding rates do not increase during this period of premigratory fattening, at least in Yellow Wagtails, nor is there yet any evidence in this species that the diet changes to a more calorie-rich one—although insectivorous *Sylvia* warblers and even *Acrocephalus* reed warblers do eat quantities of sugar-rich berries of the shrubs *Salvadora* and *Lantana*. Wagtails start to fatten immediately moult has finished, so the energy they first put into replacing their plumage is transferred without any necessary change in the feeding regime.

Birds probably depart across the desert immediately they finish fattening, for they are then so obese as to fall easy prey to hawks. Theoretical calculations show that a small land bird will burn about 0·6gm of fat for every 200km it flies, and the figures obtained in practice, by difference between average weights at departure and at landfall in various trans-Saharan migrants, confirm this.

Equatorial seabird routines

M. P. Harris

Although the Galapagos Islands were first brought to the attention of naturalists by Darwin's theories on the evolution of the various species of finches, mockingbirds and tortoises, the seabirds of the area are also of great interest and have been the subject of much study in the last two decades. The islands have a great variety of seabird species, including some groups typical of cold water and not normally associated with islands actually on the equator. Only in Galapagos can purely tropical species, such as frigatebirds and tropicbirds, be seen nesting side-by-side with cold-loving albatrosses. Certainly nowhere else do penguins occur on the equator—indeed there is one small nesting colony actually north of the equator which lays the myth that penguins do not occur in the northern hemisphere. Within a hundred miles there is a colony of Sooty or Wideawake Terns *Sterna fuscata*—such a conservative warm-water species that it is used in marine ornithology as an indicator of tropical blue water. What allows this mixing of avifaunas?

Deserts of the Sea

The distribution of most species of seabirds is governed to

a great extent by the temperature of the sea. This does not mean that the individual birds cannot tolerate a wider range of temperature but rather that the animals on which the various species feed have restricted ranges tied in with, among other factors, the sea-temperature. This holds for large fish, such as flying fish which are eaten by many tropical birds, the krill beloved of antarctic penguins and the minute animals picked off the surface of the water by storm petrels. Many species migrate across inhospitable regions but rarely stop there to feed. Manx Shearwaters *Puffinus puffinus* from Britain migrate to the temperate waters off Brazil, the Great Shearwater *P. gravis* from Tristan da Cunha and Sooty Shearwater *P. griseus* from sub-antarctica go to the northern Pacific and Atlantic Oceans. The three species cross several thousand miles of warm water and have evolved the ability to cross these areas without stopping rather than the skills needed to find food in oceans which have been called 'the deserts of the sea'.

Tropical seabirds are to be expected in Galapagos, but species such as the endemic penguin *Spheniscus mendiculus* can survive only in certain areas which are influenced by the cold Humboldt Current. This current flows northwards from about 38° S off central Chile to near the Peru–Ecuador border, where it turns westwards to run to and past the Galapagos, having a profound effect on the islands. Off Peru the current flows at some half a knot, but the speed increases to two knots during the 600 mile passage from the continent to Galapagos. This current carried out the ancestral stock which gave rise to Galapagos's unique marine and land iguanas and giant tortoises, and it also allows cold-water-specialised seabirds to visit the islands. Water temperatures are some 10° C lower than would normally be expected in these tropical latitudes. The cold water does not come from the sub-antarctic, for if it did the temperature of the current would gradually rise as it progressed northwards and mixed with the warmer waters. Instead there is a marked uniformity of temperature throughout the several-thousand-mile run of the current. The lower temperatures are due to the upwelling of deeper waters caused by the predominantly offshore winds in coastal Peru and Chile.

Upwelling

Normally there is little mixing of seawater in a vertical direction. The sea is heated by the sun and the resulting warm water is slightly less dense than the cold water, and so stays on the surface. However when the winds are offshore they push this warm water out to sea and this allows the deeper water to upwell. On exposure to sunlight the nutrient-rich water is an ideal solution for plant growth and soon there is a flush of phyto-plankton (plants), soon followed by an increase in zoo-plankton feeding on them. These in turn are eaten by fish and fish by birds. The Humboldt Current supports the world's largest fishery and also enormous concentrations of birds—even if the numbers have dramatically declined as man has removed million upon million of tons of fish—all due to the offshore winds.

Galapagos has three seabirds which have colonised the islands by passage up this current. Two of these are storm petrels which, though not restricted to Galapagos, are endemic to the Humboldt Current. One—the White-vented or Elliot's Storm Petrel *Oceanites gracilis* (probably evolved from the migratory Wilson's Storm Petrel *O. oceanicus*), remains one of the last seabirds whose nest has yet to be discovered. The third species is the Galapagos Penguin which has obviously evolved from the Humboldt Penguin *S. humboldti*, which itself is the second most northerly penguin occurring only 600 miles south of the equator. Presumably some venturesome, or perhaps unlucky, group of Humboldt Penguins swam or were carried along the current to the islands, found conditions suitable for both survival and breeding and, over an unknown number of generations, changed into the Galapagos population now extant. Apart from the Galapagos species being much smaller (a common phenomenon of both tropical and insular animals) the two species are very similar—the only differences being that the white markings around the head and on the sides of the body are much less pronounced in the smaller species. Relatively little is known of the Galapagos Penguin for it is not only rare—just a few thousand individuals—but is mainly nocturnal in its comings and goings at the breeding sites. Also it nests underneath rough lava flows in inaccessible areas and does not congregate in large colonies.

Endemics

Four other species—all endemic to these islands—are allied to species which are associated with cold waters, but in no case are we sure how they colonised Galapagos. These are the Waved Albatross *Diomedea irrorata*, Flightless Cormorant *Nannopterum harrisi*, Lava Gull *Larus fuliginosus* and Swallow-tailed Gull *Creagrus furcatus*. Although albatrosses bring to mind pictures of southern icy wastes, three species live in the temperate North Pacific and another in the tropics.

The Waved Albatross is restricted to Hood Island in Galapagos where some 12,000 pairs nest. Unlike the gulls and cormorant, this species has a very regular annual breeding cycle —eggs always being laid in April and May. The incubation and fledging periods are so long, 60 and 167 days respectively, that the last young do not leave until the end of the year. The adults then immediately leave the area and migrate south-wards down the Humboldt Current, to moult off Central

Page 89 (*above*) Millions of Yellow Wagtails, this is a Grey-headed *Motacilla flava thunbergi*, gather at Lake Chad in Nigeria prior to their migration across the desert in spring; (*below*) a female Great Frigate-bird broods its chicks on the Galapagos. There they have adopted a less-than-annual breeding routine

Page 90 (*above*) The only member of its family to cross the Equator, the Galapagos Penguin is endemic to those islands; (*below*) maintenance of the pair bond is of crucial importance to the survival of the young in a species like the North Atlantic Gannet which ranges so far in search of food

Peru. Moult is of critical importance for many seabirds and these albatrosses sometimes have difficulty in replacing all their wing feathers in this short interval. Some birds which have reared a chick do not have time to moult all the primary feathers and are forced to leave one (usually) or two (rarely) old feathers unreplaced. If time is again too short the next year, then one primary may again have to be left unreplaced— but this is always a different one so that there is no chance of a feather becoming so worn as to be useless.

Even when nesting these birds have ample time to feed well away from the islands. During incubation each adult sits on the egg for 19 days without a break and during this time its mate can forage for large squid (which sometimes weigh as much as the albatross, so are presumably found dead) and herring-type fish over vast distances. Even when they have a chick, each adult only returns to feed it once every four to six days. Despite their vast potential feeding ranges, the birds always remain within the influence of the Humboldt Current. The only concession they make to the tropics is to flap more and glide less than other albatrosses. They are forced to do this as there is less wind near the equator than in high latitudes.

Flightless Cormorant

The Flightless Cormorant is another species whose life is governed by cold water, but this finds that even the Humboldt Current is not cold enough or, more likely, that it is not sufficiently rich in food. However additional cold water is brought to the islands by the Cromwell Current which runs west to east across the Pacific underneath and contrary to the Humboldt Current. When it meets the most western of the Galapagos Islands its progress is halted by the mighty volcano of Fernandina and the water is forced to rise 10,000 feet in a matter of miles. This water may bring the surface temperature to as low as 15° C—compared to 28° C in the centre of the archipelago. This cold water with its very high productivity supports a high concentration of birds, whales and fish. Here and only here is found the Flightless Cormorant whose total population is 700–800 pairs concentrated along 200 miles of coastline.

Most of the penguins also breed in this area, but these birds do swim to other parts of the archipelago when not nesting. Flightless Cormorants do not, and must be among the most sedentary of all birds. None have ever been recorded more than a mile outside the breeding range. Presumably the original colonists could fly and the species has since become flightless due to the rich supply of food and the lack of enemies. Flightlessness has some advantages: for instance the birds can become much heavier, which makes diving easier; but it also has hidden drawbacks. The birds must feed near to the colonies or they cannot carry back enough octopuses, eels and other fish to feed the young even if the food is available— swimming is far slower than flying. In addition, as with all cormorants, the waterproofing of the feathers is inefficient and the birds have to come ashore periodically to dry their feathers. The price of these specialisations is a very restricted distribution tied to a very rich feeding area of shallow reefs close to good nesting places and easy landings. The restricted distribution makes the species susceptible to disturbance, and there is some concern over the possibility that net-fishing for lobsters might be started in the area. Such nets could easily result in the extinction of this bird. As far as is known the species has never been more widespread or more common. Indeed, it may once have been even scarcer, as Darwin missed seeing either it or the penguin despite spending several days in areas where they are now found.

Lost Ancestry

The Lava Gull has probably evolved from the North American Laughing Gull *L. atricilla* which is a migrant to the islands, whereas the Swallow-tailed Gull has become so specialised that we cannot even speculate as to its ancestry. For this reason the latter species is put into a monotypic genus —a genus of just one species—whereas the close relationships of most other gulls are admitted by putting them together in the genus *Larus*.

As a group, gulls are neither widespread nor common in the tropics where their ecological places are taken by a variety of terns. The reasons for this scarcity are doubtless many and varied, but only in Galapagos do gulls nest close to frigatebirds. Although quite capable of catching their own food, frigates also chase other seabirds and harry them until they regurgitate their last meal which the frigatebird then eats. The Lava and Swallow-tailed Gulls have solved this problem of the loss of food in different ways: the Lava Gull, a scavenger which competes with the frigatebird for food, has become dark all over, to blend with the dark lava which so characterises the Galapagos coastline. The Swallow-tailed Gull has become a nocturnal feeder, spending the days either sitting on the egg or sleeping. As darkness falls the gulls fly out to feed on squid and fish which are much commoner at the surface by night than by day. Thus in addition to being safer the species can take advantage of an unexploited food resource, for surprisingly few seabirds feed at night. The young are also fed entirely at night; any adult returning late with fish for its chick will lose it to frigatebirds, and an adult which frequently made this mistake would be unlikely to leave any offspring, so the trait would soon be eliminated from the population. Adapta-

93

tions to this nocturnal existence include very large eyes, very ungull-like calls, a pale tip to the beak and a patch of white feathers at the base of the bill. Chicks need to peck at these light areas to stimulate the adults to feed them—just as young Herring Gulls *L. argentatus* are only fed if they peck at the red releaser spot on the adult's lower mandible.

Most gulls lay a clutch of three eggs and have three brood patches where heat is passed from the adult to the eggs during incubation. The Swallow-tailed Gull lays a single egg for the clutch and has two brood patches. Its peculiar feeding regime probably prevents the adult collecting enough food to rear three young. It can, however, successfully incubate two eggs and very rarely, perhaps once in 5,000 cases, lays two eggs. It is probably just completing the evolution of a single-egg clutch. Experiments where pairs are given two young have shown that sometimes they can rear two young, so why do they not normally lay two eggs? Unlike some other gulls the adults look after the young for some time after they have fledged and it may be difficult for a pair to look after more than one. After nesting, adults and young leave the archipelago and, like the albatrosses, go to Peru to moult.

Year-Round Breeding

Among seabird biologists Galapagos is well known for the fact that some species breed more frequently than once a year. Similar routines are known from a few other islands, all near the equator. In many birds the changes in day-length are the most important cues in bringing the adults into breeding condition. On the equator, day-length is constant throughout the year so it is possible in Galapagos to look for other factors. Swallow-tailed Gulls can be found nesting in large numbers in all months of the year and ringing has shown that each individual pair breeds at intervals of about nine months between consecutive layings. However, the level of nesting at any one colony is not uniform, the peaks and troughs of laying again being about nine months apart. These peaks are not related to any external factor, like food, which could conceivably also have a nine-month cycle as colonies on neighbouring islands have peaks at different times. If the whole Galapagos population is considered as a unit then the level of nesting is more or less constant. In this way the minimum strain is put on the food supply, assuming that the supply is either uniform or unpredictable. All the available evidence suggests the latter.

Equatorial Seasons

Although the islands are on the equator they do have regular seasons, because the northern boundary of the Humboldt Current moves north and south. When the islands are influenced by cold water the weather tends to be cloudy and rather cold, whereas at other times the more northern islands may escape from the cold water and are influenced by warm waters from the Gulf of Panama. In any one place there is an annual variation of 5° C in the surface sea temperature. However, the regular movements of the current are easily upset and there is hardly such a thing as a typical year.

Sampling of the plankton has shown no regular seasonal fluctuation in the food for the smaller seabirds. It could be that the sampling technique was inadequate, as it is very difficult to sample mid-water fish, but the facts that some seabirds nest throughout the year while others have annual cycles, though these vary from island to island, suggest that there is no great seasonal flush of food. If there were, then there would quickly be a synchronisation of nesting, both by individuals of any one species and by the different species, at some time of the year—just as happens in Britain.

95

Synchronised Breeding

Synchronisation of breeding does occur in the tropics and is brought about by two separate influences. Some species, like the Swallow-tailed Gull, are very social birds and seem to have a regular non-annual breeding cycle regardless of what is happening to the environment. In this case there must be some great advantage to the individual pair in nesting when everyone else does; perhaps it is protection against frigate-birds or other predators. However, in contrast, synchronisation may be forced on a species. Audubon's Shearwaters have their nesting synchronised by the availability of food. The egg is so large (up to one-fifth the weight of the bird) that the female has difficulty in finding enough food to produce it and, if food is short, she may not be able to lay. When feeding conditions are good, indicated by large and regular feeds being given to young already in the colony, there are always birds coming into breeding condition and laying eggs. However, once feeds to the young become small and erratic, laying immediately stops and the backlog of birds apparently wanting to lay but unable to do so builds up. In times of severe shortage the young die, eggs already laid are deserted, and all the birds leave the area. When food is again plentiful, all these waiting adults lay more or less at the same time, giving a large peak of breeding; the longer the shortage, the larger the peak. Thus breeding is controlled directly by the amount of food available at the time and there is no chance of birds timing their nesting so that they will have young when food is most abundant—which is the case in British and most other temperate seabirds. All the Audubon's Shearwaters can do is to lay when they can and hope for the best. They may live some twenty years, so a failure to nest even for a year is of little consequence. It does not pay them to risk their own survival in trying to rear young under impossible conditions.

Replacement Clutches

So far we have been considering the factors which influence the time of nesting. But there is another fundamental question: what stops birds nesting? If the environment is unpredictable then there will be occasional long periods when conditions are good, yet none of these birds is double-brooded. Once they finish nesting they leave the colonies. Audubon's Shearwater will not even lay again if the egg is lost immediately after it is laid. Most gulls relay several times in a season if they lose their clutches, though the Swallow-tailed Gull is a partial exception as only one pair in five or six relay even if their neighbours are still only starting to nest. Clearly something is preventing these birds from continually breeding. The most obvious possible reason is that the gonads need to recuperate between breeding attempts. However, as many seabirds only lay a single egg per cycle it is unlikely that the gonads need to 'rest'. In the shearwater, successful pairs relay nine months after the first laying but the interval between layings is slightly shorter (8 months) in those whose chick dies, and even shorter ($6\frac{1}{2}$ months) in those which lose their egg. These differences are due to a constant interval between the end of one attempt, whether the loss of a newly laid egg or the fledging of a young, and the start of the next. This strongly suggests that the pairs are breeding as quickly as possible, but are prevented from shortening the gap by something unrelated to the last nesting. Again this rules out gonad recuperation. More likely it is the need to moult. In most birds adults do not replace their main wing and tail feathers at the same time as they are feeding young. In some seabirds this moult does just start when they

97

have large young, but only in the middle of the wing; not in the outer primaries. In species which nest non-annually the moult fills the whole time between breeding cycles, and birds coming back to reclaim nest-sites are still completing the growth of the outer primaries. It is possible that the moult is adapted to a poor food supply, making it advantageous to spread the moult over as long a period as possible. It is difficult to decide this 'chicken and egg' impasse, but as food is unpredictable it must surely pay the bird to moult and be ready to breed as soon as possible.

Even with the very high adult survival of these tropical birds it still seems wasteful not to replace a lost egg. Possibly raising young is so difficult that the adult must be in absolute peak condition for finding and carrying back the food. Natural selection may well have favoured the adults which had the newest feathers when feeding young. It does appear that the main factor preventing more rapid breeding is the need to replace worn feathers.

Gannets and boobies

Bryan Nelson

Gannets and boobies form a small but picturesque and highly successful group of seabirds. Comprising a mere nine species, if one accords specific status to each of the three gannets (Atlantic, Cape or African and Australasian), they yet manage to inhabit a wide range of feeding and breeding habitats throughout the world. Thick black ropes of piqueros or Peruvian Boobies lace the misty surface of the cold Humboldt in the Pacific, and nest on bare, precipitous slopes of islands within sight of the Andean foothills; the icy waters on both sides of the Atlantic, and the North Sea are the productive foraging areas of the Atlantic Gannet which nests in huge colonies often on precipitous cliffs; the Cape Gannet breeds only near the southern tip of Africa and the Australasian Gannet mainly off the New Zealand coast.

The tropical blue-water belts of the Indian, Pacific and Atlantic are quartered by the highly pelagic Red-footed and Masked Boobies, the former nesting in trees and bushes on thousands of small oceanic islands, the latter inhabiting a range of ground habitats on the same islands; the Brown Booby, also a pan-tropical species, often shares the same areas as the other two, and nests on slopes and cliffs; the Blue-footed Booby, the most 'bobo', or dunce-like, of all the boobies, has a rather odd, discontinuous distribution off central America, the west coast of South America (out to the

99

Galapagos) and in the Gulf of California, and is another ground-nester, while the rarest and most restricted of all, Abbott's Booby, breeds only on the forest trees of the Central Plateau of Christmas Island in the Indian Ocean. Where two or more species nest on the same island, they choose different niches. Almost never does one find two kinds of boobies intermingled. Commonly, three booby species nest on the same island, very rarely (as in the Revillagigedos) four. None of the three species of gannets breeds with any other sulid.

Numerous Tree-nesters

The most numerous sulid is probably the Red-footed Booby, of which there are likely to be many more than 2 million pairs in the world. One of the reasons for this is its tree-nesting habit, which protects it from the depredations of natives. The two ground-nesting boobies are easy prey and have certainly suffered massive losses in the past. I estimate that there are about 2 million Brown and Masked Boobies, the former slightly commoner, and around 1 million Peruvian Boobies (the figure may be lower as a result of the 1972 crash, see below). Despite its highly restricted distribution, the Peruvian Booby has frequently numbered around 2 million pairs (this reflects the astonishing number of anchovies in the Humboldt Current). No other sulid approaches even half a million. The figures are: Atlantic Gannet, 197,000 pairs; Cape Gannet, 125,000; Blue-footed Booby, perhaps 100,000; Australasian Gannet, 25,000; and Abbott's Booby, 2,000 or 3,000.

The moral seems to be that, to be numerous, a species has to achieve either a very wide distribution in the poorer waters (which predominate in the world) or to carve itself a niche in one of the very rich feeding areas. On a reduced scale, the moral applies to the three gannets, for the Atlantic Gannet inhabits the richest feeding area and is the most numerous, the Australasian the poorest and has fewest individuals. In world terms, a total population of something between 7 and 10 million pairs of gannets and boobies is considerably less than that of some other seabird families (for example, terns, penguins, shearwaters, auks), but considering their large size and the fact that most of them inhabit relatively impoverished zones, it is not a bad score.

Colonial Density

The sulids vary enormously in the nature and size of their colonies. The most densely nesting species is the Cape Gannet (up to six pairs per square metre); the other two gannets and the Peruvian Booby are not far behind. The least colonial sulid is Abbott's Booby, many of which nest solitarily in the jungle of Christmas Island. The rest fall between. The general principle is that the species which nest most densely are also those which show least variation in density; the Atlantic Gannet is a good example, nesting at a highly standard density wherever topography allows. By contrast, Brown Boobies, which commonly nest several metres apart, range from nesting cheek by jowl to nesting almost solitarily. It would be a mistake to imagine that density is determined simply by the availability of suitable sites. Often this has little to do with it, the advantages of the observed spacing being largely social. On the other hand, sites certainly are (or were) scarce on the Peruvian Islands and those of south-west Africa; one has to take the species' entire breeding biology into account before interpreting the nature of the selection pressures shaping nesting density.

So far as the size of colonies is concerned, all sulids can, as it were, afford to nest in large colonies because all are capable of foraging relatively far from the colony and so can draw on vast feeding areas. By contrast, cormorants cannot form huge colonies except where food is superabundant (as in the Humboldt) because they do not fly far for food, and the area immediately around the colony cannot usually support more than a relatively small number. Nevertheless, colony size among sulids does vary enormously from the largest (around 350,000 pairs of Peruvian Boobies on a Peruvian island) down to colonies of two pairs in the cases of several boobies and of our own Atlantic Gannet.

If we consider 'typical' colony size, for each species, we find that the ones that nest the most densely also form the largest colonies. While this is readily understandable where space is scarce and food abundant, it is less so where both commodities are plentiful, and in such cases the advantages of large and dense colonies are again probably social ones, concerned with the timing of breeding. The three gannets form an interesting trio with regard to the number and size of their colonies. Since they are so extremely alike, they might be expected to approximate in these respects, but in fact the differences in their environments dictate otherwise. The world population of the Atlantic Gannet occupies thirty-four colonies, a common size being around 5,000–10,000 pairs and the largest (St Kilda) numbering 59,000 pairs. The Cape Gannet crams all its members into six colonies, the 'typical' size of which is much larger, the biggest (Ichaboe) being 100,000 pairs. The Australasian Gannet has some twenty-five colonies, none of them larger than about 5,000 pairs. Again the richer food supply of the Atlantic and Cape Gannets probably has much to do with it.

Food and Breeding Density

The fact that the nature of the feeding and breeding areas dictates much of the species' breeding biology becomes clearer when we look at breeding ecology. Ecology, of course, is the relationship between a species and its total environment, including other species. The fundamental relationship between a gannet or a booby and its environment concerns food. While it is obvious that a bird's physical features, such as size, shape, beak and feet, are closely correlated with its food, it is not immediately apparent that the number of eggs it lays, or the timing of its breeding, is similarly related, down to the finest details. Two boobies and a gannet between them illustrate the full range of adaptations I have in mind. These species are the Red-footed Booby, the Peruvian Booby and our own Atlantic Gannet.

The Red-foot has a wide distribution on oceanic islands throughout the tropics and nests in colonies of variable, but usually fairly modest, size (a few thousand pairs often fairly widely dispersed in small groups) in trees or bushes; mangroves are much favoured. It forages up to about 300 miles from its breeding colony and is in fact the most pelagic of all boobies except, perhaps, the Masked. It catches mainly flying fish and squids, which are typical inhabitants of the warm, relatively impoverished 'blue' waters of the tropical oceans. Two characteristic features of such areas are that the climate is more or less aseasonal and that food is occasionally and quite unpredictably extremely scarce for a time. Why it becomes so nobody knows, but we may guess that it has to do with complex oceanographic phenomena such as temperature change and currents. In any event, this is the background against which in such localities the Red-foot has evolved its entire breeding biology.

The Galapagos is a good example and the following features may be seen as direct adaptations to this food regime. First, egg-laying may occur at any time of year, which makes sense if one time is no better than another. Moreover, bursts of egg laying are actually linked to periods of relative abundance of food, probably because at such times the males are better able to cope with the demands of territorial and nest-building behaviour, and the females with the production of an egg. Of course an erratic food supply means that the young may be growing just at the time when food becomes short, and many may starve, but this is a risk which cannot be eliminated no matter what the bird does.

It has however, evolved some helpful adaptations. It keeps its clutch size strictly to one egg, which is relatively large and so gives the newly hatched chick bigger reserves, so that it can survive longer periods without food if it should be unlucky enough to hatch at a bad time. The chick has evolved a slow growth-rate, which is 'built in', and so increases its capacity to resist long periods of semi-starvation. The adults have evolved the habit of feeding their young for an exceptionally long period (up to a year) after the latter have become fully grown and free-flying. This maximises their chances of becoming proficient hunters under the difficult conditions which they may face. Despite all this, breeding success is extremely low. In some years less than 10 per cent of eggs laid result in free-flying young; the remainder are deserted during a period of acute food shortage, or else the chicks die from starvation or predation.

To underline the fact that all this is an environmental effect, one need only study the Red-foot in a part of its range where food conditions are more seasonal, plentiful and predictable, such as Christmas Island in the Indian Ocean. Here the whole picture is far different. Breeding is seasonal; eggs are smaller;

young grow quicker and breeding success is much higher.

The Peruvian Booby stands in most striking contrast. It has a restricted distribution off Peru, where it nests in vast, dense colonies. Its food supply is normally near at hand and super-abundant but, at intervals of roughly seven years, disaster strikes: a double phenomenon, the failure of the upwelling of cold water off Peru and less importantly a southwards exten-sion of an equatorial flow of warm water from Central America, drives the anchovies into deeper layers where they are inaccessible to the birds. Because the second of these two happenings typically occurs at Christmas, the term 'El niño' (the child) is often loosely used to embrace the whole phenom-enon. The spawning rhythm of the anchovies means that fish are usually fewest between about May and August. Against this background, the Red-foot's regime would be disastrous, but the Peruvian Booby has evolved appropriate responses.

It lays chiefly around December; its clutch comprises two, three or even four eggs; nevertheless all the young grow quickly and breeding success is high. This leads to a rapid build-up in numbers, but the niño years cause terrific mortal-ity of both young and old, the birds dying in millions. Thus the population is vastly reduced, only to rise again before the next disaster.

Seasonal Patterns

The Atlantic Gannet, too, has a superabundant food supply, but unlike the Peruvian Booby occupies a highly seasonal environment. In particular, the length of the breeding season is squeezed at both ends—by the short days and stormy weather of winter and by the gales of autumn. Gannets have gone in for a shortened growth period, made possible by the abundance of herring and mackerel during summer. They manage to produce a chick which, at a maximum weight of 4,500gm, is one and a half times as heavy as the adult and by far the heaviest sulid. Most of the weight is due to thick deposits of fat. Despite this, the chick fledges after only 91 days in the nest, compared with as much as 150 in the Red-foot. Moreover, the youngster severs its ties with its parents in one step, by jumping off the cliff ledge and not returning. It thus reduces its period of dependence and so shortens its development period still more, at the cost of relinquishing the valuable safeguard of parental subsidy during the vital days or weeks when it is acquiring the difficult art of plunge-diving. Presumably the point of all this is to reduce the risk of being caught 'unfinished' at a time of rapidly deteriorating weather. If all goes well, young gannets are safely on their way south by August or early September, but up to 60 per cent die in those first months. This reverses the pattern of mortality found in the Red-foot, but then the environmental conditions are reversed.

Division of Labour

In these three examples one can glimpse the nature of the selection pressures which have shaped breeding ecology. Of course all the other sulids have their own problems too. The Masked and Brown Boobies, tropical blue-water species, are in many respects similar to the Red-foot. They lay clutches of two eggs, which may seem contrary, but in fact end up with broods of one, because the older chick evicts its young sibling, which quickly dies. They do this as an inbuilt response long before there is any competition for the available food. The Blue-foot is, with the exception of the Peruvian which in-habits a specially favourable area, the only sulid which rears more than a single chick per brood. In the Galapagos it does

Page 107 (*above*) Rarest of all the gannets and boobies, Abbott's Booby is found only on Christmas Island; (*below*) highly localised in its winter haunts, the Knot is one of the most numerous birds on the major British estuaries

Page 108 Mass ringing of Sand Martins under the guidance of the BTO ringing scheme raised the recovery rate of the species dramatically as ringers began to catch each other's birds

this by virtue of an unusual division of labour between the sexes linked to a high degree of sexual dimorphism. The male is only two-thirds as large and heavy as the female and has specialised in diving into the shallow water near its breeding place. It is thus able to feed the small young at frequent intervals (they do not need much at a time). When they become larger and are able to go for longer periods without food, the female takes over. She is able to bring larger amounts though she needs longer foraging trips.

Migrations

Breeding leads, eventually, to the recruitment of young adults to the population. Before this can happen, the young must undergo a variable period of maturation. Mostly, this occurs at least partly away from the breeding place. The young of the tropical boobies (Brown, Masked and Red-footed) wander extensively, up to 6,000km from their birthplace. Some return to their home island, whilst others settle down elsewhere. Usually they do not breed until their third year. Young gannets of all three 'species' migrate. Our own birds begin by swimming southwards for a week or two, after which they are light enough to complete their journey on the wing. Some go as far as the Gulf of Guinea, where they overlap with young Cape Gannets which have similarly migrated to lower latitudes from the south-western tip of Africa. There they stay for a year or two before working their way north again.

Young Australasian Gannets migrate across the Tasman sea from New Zealand to the south and east coasts of Australia. In May and June a stream of young Atlantic Gannets in the immature piebald plumage return off the western seaboard of Europe and along the west coast of Britain. Many, attracted by the exciting activity at colonies into whose orbits they stray, stay on and eventually breed. There is massive interchange of recruits between colonies on the west, though once a bird has bred, it remains in that particular colony for life. Our own gannets are slower to reach maturity than the other species, probably because it is important for them to learn local fishing areas. Males take longer than females, probably because the stress is greatest on them (they have to compete for a site and undertake extremely arduous behaviour in its defence).

Breeding Behaviour

Breeding behaviour is complex in all sulids. One should think of it in terms of an elaborate communication system. Messages are conveyed from partner to partner, or from neighbour to neighbour, by stereotyped postures and movements, or displays. These often employ the most striking physical features of the birds, such as their brightly coloured faces or feet. The messages have to do with territory, sex, or collaboration in routine duties. Thus, a site-owning male has to be recognisable as such. It is no good simply standing on the site; if that were sufficient sign of ownership, the rightful male, were he to return and find an interloper on his nest, would have to accept the usurper. If, on the other hand, an arriving bird was to attack a bird on site, how would anybody know who was the rightful owner? The owner has to have a conspicuous signal; then there is little chance of wasteful strife. Every sulid has, in fact, a site-ownership display which is undoubtedly recognised and acted upon by other individuals. The exact nature of the display varies, but it is always conspicuous and stereotyped.

Similarly, it is extremely useful for a bird to indicate its sexual status, to encourage pair formation. All sulids have sexually motivated 'advertising' displays. Once the pair have come together, they must forge an adequate bond so that copulation can occur and the duties of incubation and chick rearing be efficiently discharged in collaboration with each other. Thus we find elaborate 'pair' displays, of which the ecstatic greeting ceremony of the gannet is a dramatic example. This and comparable kinds of behaviour are called 'ritualised' and are quite different from ordinary non-communicatory behaviour such as preening, yawning, scratching, sleeping, defaecating, bathing and so on. Young sulids do rather little in their first month or so except for begging, feeding and sleeping. Later, they begin to exercise and in many species begin to help defend their parents' territory, before finally migrating or dispersing.

Diving for Food

Breeding behaviour is more easily studied than feeding behaviour. All sulids are plunge divers, to which mode of feeding they are adapted by streamlined shape, closed nostrils, forward vision and protective air-sacs. Although all of them have similarly shaped beaks with saw edges, long narrow wings and cigar-shaped bodies, close examination shows that in wing-loading, and in the mechanical properties of their beaks, they form a nicely graded series in all areas in which they overlap; this series incorporates the sexual dimorphisms too. In other words, if one has, say, four sulid species in the same general feeding area, they will differ in their feeding capacities. Too little is known about prey preferences to match this morphological data, but presumably the two are correlated.

The heaviest sulid is the Atlantic Gannet, which plunges from heights of between 200 and 150 feet, usually falling simply by gravity and using its wings to control the angle and direction. It hits the water with terrific impact and though it penetrates more deeply than any other sulid it can hardly go much deeper than 10 or 20 feet and is rarely submerged for more than about seven seconds. The idea that it stuns the fish by transmitted shock is not fanciful, for it has been authentically demonstrated that a large pike can be stunned by hitting the water above it with the blade of an oar. Gannets can hunt also, by diving from a swimming position, or by wading for sand-eels. They must benefit from fishing communally, otherwise they surely would not have evolved such dazzling plumage, which certainly attracts conspecifics and leads to the formation of spectacular diving flocks.

The basic technique of hunting is similar in all sulids, but two (the Blue-footed and Brown Boobies) have evolved true co-operative hunting: actual co-ordinating signals are produced, which lead to deliberately concerted action by the group. Red-footed Boobies, in particular, take much of their prey on the wing.

In many ways the rarest sulid of all, Abbott's Booby, is the most fascinating, for its restriction to the rain forest of the Central Plateau of Christmas Island is particularly evocative. It is unusual, too, in having a particularly large egg, slow growth and extended dependence (as a juvenile) on its parents. This prolongs the breeding season so much that it can breed only once every two years. Therefore, as its population is tiny (about 2,000–3,000 pairs), it is peculiarly vulnerable. The underlying reasons for its particular breeding regime can only be guessed at, but the evidence suggests that it is adapted to feeding in an area of upwelling off Java Head, which entails long foraging journeys. This means a relatively low feeding-rate for the chick. Its subsequent dependence is in part due to the dangers of the jungle-top environment and, perhaps, to the time necessary to learn the feeding area. The former means that fledging must be delayed until the chick is fully competent, for if it once tumbles to the ground it is doomed.

It is pleasant to report that, despite the large-scale clearing of Christmas Island prior to phosphate mining, the Government of Australia (which owns the island) is now alive to the great value and rarity of this lovely island's avifauna and has made recommendations which, if carried out, will safeguard it.

The new bird ringer

Robert Spencer

Like the butterfly-collector, the bird-watcher endured for years the reputation of being mildly eccentric: he was a cartoon character, harmless enough but a trifle absurd, and not to be emulated. Times change. Today bird-watching is fast becoming both a national pastime and a growth industry, and the old image has gone for ever.

This is not yet true of the bird ringer. He remains a member of a very tiny minority—there are fewer than 2,000 ringers in the whole of Britain and Ireland—rarely understood and sometimes the victim of ignorance, not yet fully accepted as a harmless, let alone valued, member of the natural history fraternity. It is easy to see why this should be, for while it is becoming quite difficult to take a country walk without encountering someone watching birds, very few people have had an opportunity to watch a ringer at work. Even more than the bird-watcher he shuns company, not because he is anti-social, but because visitors disturb the birds and distract his own concentration. He works unobtrusively whenever possible, often operating at dawn and dusk when birds tend to be less wary. The results of bird ringing are often so interesting and important that they are mentioned in the general press and on radio and television; but the methods used are not known or understood nearly so well.

Perhaps because most people object strongly to seeing birds such as Goldfinches and Linnets caught for caging (an illegal practice which nevertheless continues) and are revolted by the thought of our country forefathers netting Skylarks and thrushes for the pot, there is an antipathy to the idea of catching birds at all. The fact that the ringer, if he is to learn anything about migration, must release the bird he catches is only partly reassuring. In the absence of an opportunity to see for themselves some people worry about the ring, finding it easy to believe that it must be a handicap to the bird.

No Handicap

Bird ringing, as we shall see, is both exacting and expensive. It seeks to find out facts about the lives of normal healthy birds, and assumes that the movements of marked individuals are typical of the population as a whole. If rings handicapped birds, preventing them from leading normal lives, the very basis of the work would be destroyed, and a great many people throughout the world would be wasting their time and money. To make sure that the birds are not handicapped, much thought and money have been expended on ring design. Special alloys are used to afford maximum strength with minimum weight, and their manufacture involves working to very close tolerances. The smallest rings used in Britain have an inside diameter of 2mm and are so light that it takes 675 of them to weigh 1oz.

Formalities

Twenty-five years ago the formalities involved in becoming a ringer were minimal: one was asked which bird books one read, which magazines, and whether one belonged to any society. Today's would-be ringer faces an apprenticeship which rarely takes less than a year and may last several. Before he can begin he has to obtain a licence from the Nature Conservancy Council (for which he has to be sponsored) and almost immediately afterwards a British Trust for Ornithology ringing permit. It is the latter which reflects his skills. He will start with a Trainee Permit, moving on when his experience and competence merit it to a probationer's class 'C' permit, and later to fully qualified ringer status with a 'B' or an 'A'. By this time he will generally have handled, under supervision, upwards of 1,000 birds. After a further two years, during which he will have continued to develop his skills and widen his experience, he will himself become eligible to start training others.

If he wishes to ring nestlings he will require an additional NCC licence and will need to undertake special training before having his BTO ringing permit endorsed with the extra authorisation. Similarly, if he wishes to use mist nets—diaphanous Terylene nets which intercept birds in flight, first introduced from Japan in 1956—he will need an additional NCC licence and must qualify with a BTO trainer to use the nets correctly.

Because a ringer very literally takes the lives of birds into his hands every time he operates (not to mention the scientific integrity of the programme), it is right that his training should be as thorough as possible, and anyone who has the right qualities to make a reliable ringer submits willingly to the discipline. Yet the system of training does have its drawbacks. Judged strictly from a scientific point of view it is desirable to have qualified ringers spaced evenly about the country—say one every twenty miles—for this would make it possible to detect and study regional differences. We know, for example, that Blackbirds are relatively sedentary in the south of

England but fairly migratory in the north of Scotland. How many similar differences remain undetected?

Ringer Distribution

An apprenticeship system which of necessity operates only in leisure hours inevitably means that training is most readily available in areas already well served by ringers. In Scotland, Wales and Ireland there are whole counties without a resident ringer, so that the trainee has to travel long distances in search of help, then maybe finding that strong winds keep the day's catch down to a handful of birds. Little wonder that only the most enthusiastic embark upon such a demanding commitment and that only the most resolute stay the course. Yet near large centres of population there may be almost too many opportunities for training, bringing its own problems.

Twenty years ago nearly all birds were caught in large wire netting traps, so bulky that ringing activities were virtually confined to back gardens. Today the average garden is much smaller and proportionately less rich in bird life, but we have the mist net, which is highly portable and has enabled the ringer to go out into the country. There he will probably look for woodland, scrub, a marshy area, a gravel pit, a sewage farm—somewhere where birds congregate and humans do not, and somewhere secure from invasion by farm animals, for the curious approach of a cow can in seconds destroy a net worth £10. In our increasingly populous islands such areas are not always easy to discover and a newly qualified ringer may have considerable difficulty in finding somewhere to work which is not already claimed by another.

Corporate Ringing

A commonly adopted solution is to share sites—a practice known as corporate ringing. A quarter of a century ago ringing was primarily a solitary occupation: a few natural-history societies claimed to ring corporately, but what this generally meant was that they drew their rings from a common stock and then used them as private individuals. The fact that they sometimes used 'society' rings when on holiday hundreds of miles from their home county did not prevent them from publishing in the county report a list of birds ringed that year.

The position today is very different. A good site is often shared by a ringing group who use a common set of rings and thus share also the not inconsiderable expenses: £100 would be an average initial outlay for such a group. The ornithological benefits may be even greater. With manning shared by members of a group, sometimes even on a duty rota basis, there may be cover on every weekend of the year, for year after year. From such intensive studies emerges a remarkably detailed picture of the bird life of the area—its comings and goings, its pairings and parental success and its mortality. Nor is activity necessarily confined to ringing: observations may supplement its findings, and vice versa, and entomologists and botanists may bring their special skills to bear on problems of food and habitat requirements. There is perhaps no better way of coming to know the ornithological potential of a site, and a number of our nature reserves first came to notice through such studies. As it has had a practical outcome this might be termed applied research, but like so much ringing it springs initially from a simple quest for knowledge. If only to keep their members informed of progress, most ringing groups publish at least a duplicated annual report and some of the more flourishing groups produce well-edited printed ones which may contain papers of international interest.

Common Ground

Sometimes the coming together of ringers is based not on a

shared locality but on a shared interest in a species or group of species. The Canada Goose enthusiasts are an example of this, and their story demonstrates better than most the difficulty of drawing firm lines between pure and applied research.

As an introduced species the Canada Goose was for long neglected by most bird-watchers, a fate suffered by most feral species. Wild or not, it so flourished that on some large estates it became an agricultural pest, requiring control. Doubtless the excess could have been culled by shooting, but this seemingly did not happen. Instead it was decided to round up some of the surplus population and to transport them to other suitable localities. This work was carried out by the staff of the Wildfowl Trust, who ringed the birds before release to find out whether or not they attempted to return to familiar waters. Unexpectedly some of the early ringing revealed long-distance movements within Britain, and gradually it became clear that in the 200 years since their introduction to Britain some Canada Geese have already developed a true migration.

What better subject could there be for a detailed ringing study, dealing with the development of migratory traditions? It was, however, far too big a problem for the lone ringer. The geese have to be caught when flightless at the height of the moult, and a big round-up on difficult terrain may require the co-ordinated efforts of 20 to 30 people, with beaters, Land Rovers and boats used to shepherd the flightless birds into a prepared corral. Latterly, too, the study has called for expeditions to recapture Canada Geese in north-east Scotland at the completion of their journey. Because the total population is still only a few thousand, and confined to a relatively small number of waters, the species offers ideal opportunities for a study of both migration and mortality based on the capture and recapture of ringed birds.

119

Cost-benefit Analysis

The first forty years of bird ringing in Britain and Ireland established that for each species the proportion of ringed birds subsequently found by members of the public is fairly constant, and generally low. Thanks to shooting, some ducks and geese may show a rate of over 20 per cent, but for song birds the return is much less, varying between about 0·3 per cent for some small warblers and 4·0 per cent for town Blackbirds. In these days of cost-benefit analysis such figures may be judged to represent a poor return on investment. Since there is no other way of obtaining the information, ringers have learned to work within these limitations but, partly in answer to them, have gradually developed three important and interconnected tenets.

1. Since the recovery rate is low, every effort should be made to learn something from the bird in the hand. There is, for example, much current interest in finding methods of ageing and sexing birds reliably, and in this connection most ringers measure the wings of birds they capture. Their measurements have shown that when fully adult a bird is likely to be a little larger than in its first year. Sometimes, where the sexes differ in wing length, it is possible to detect differences in their migrations. Many ringers weigh their birds, discovering that there is an annual weight cycle, and that weight is often a clue to the physiological preparedness of the bird to migrate. For some ringers moult is now a subject of absorbing interest, for we have come increasingly to realise that, like migration and raising a family, it is for birds another time of great physiological stress, lasting several weeks, which must somehow be fitted into the annual cycle.

2. A quarter of a century ago most ringers worked solely in

the hope that members of the public would recover at least some of their birds. If they trapped in their gardens and caught a bird already wearing one of their rings it was often released unexamined with the disappointed comment, 'It's only a retrap.' Today it is realised that retraps may be quite as valuable as recoveries, or even more so, for they provide a chance to reweigh a bird at a different time in its annual or diurnal cycle, to re-examine its plumage to assess how fast moult has progressed, or to carry out similar investigations. Indeed many modern ringing studies are based primarily on retraps, and if a bird is recovered this is regarded as a welcome bonus.

3. Though the public may recover only a tiny proportion of ringed birds (usually when they die), ringers who make frequent big catches often capture or 'control' birds which have been ringed elsewhere. This naturally happens most often with species which are highly gregarious for at least a part of the year, so the Canada Goose ringers benefit in this way. However, as a planned technique, 'controls' have been best exploited by ringers specialising in shore waders—and once again, as we shall see, the operation is dependent on highly co-ordinated teamwork.

Cannon Nets

Second only to the mist net in shaping the pattern of modern ringing activities is a device known as the cannon net. Briefly, small explosive charges in a number of specially designed cannons are fired electrically, propelling projectiles which pull a large net into the air. The back of the net is anchored securely to the ground but, on the cannons being fired, the leading edge describes an arc through the air. As soon as the net is fully extended it drops to the ground, to cover an area which may measure as much as 90 feet by 40 feet. When fired over a compact flock of shore waders, the net may take over 1,000 birds at a time. To handle such large numbers it is imperative that a well-rehearsed team of ringers and helpers is on hand, perhaps thirty strong, each knowing exactly what his or her part is throughout the operation. For from the moment that the firing button is pressed, speed is essential.

Using such equipment, and starting from a pioneer study on the Wash, British ringers have, in a series of expeditions to recapture the birds they have ringed, traced the migration of the Knot northwards via Iceland to Greenland and Ellesmere Land, and southwards via Morocco to West Africa. Big catches of ringed birds have been made in areas so under-populated that perhaps only once in a decade could one expect a recovery to be reported by a local inhabitant.

Costly Business

From the very earliest days of ringing in Britain in 1909, ringers have always paid for the rings they use and have provided all their own equipment. To the initial outlay mentioned earlier must be added an annual permit fee, the bill for rings (even the smallest ones nowadays cost over 1·5p each and the largest ones 11p) and the costs of replacements: mist nets are too fragile to have a long life. It is doubtful whether any keen ringer has ever attempted to cost the time he gives to his hobby, or his true transport bill. Maybe this is a good thing for the sum would undoubtedly be a high one. In recognition of this very generous support the Ringing and Migration Committee of the BTO—the body responsible for managing the ringing scheme—imposes as few restrictions as possible on the freedom of ringers to ring the species which most interest them.

These interests, and indeed the motivations of ringers, vary enormously. There are scientifically minded ringers who know exactly what they are trying to achieve with their ringing and work steadfastly over a number of years to attain their goal. At the other extreme are people who derive their satisfaction from the privilege of close contact with birds afforded by a ringing permit, or for whom ringing, like stalking a bird with a telephoto lens, is at least partly a sublimation of man's hunting instinct. To be healthy the ringing scheme needs both kinds of ringer—like privates and generals—and in the right proportion, for if every ringer wanted to appeal for co-operation in his own pet study, and to analyse the results, chaos would ensue.

Regardless of motivation, most modern ringers think of themselves as conservationists. Ringing, they will point out, has shown that the Ospreys so devotedly protected in Scotland are then shot on their way to winter quarters in Africa; that British-bred Redpolls are apt to end their days in the aviaries of Belgian bird-fanciers and that countless British and Irish pipits and wagtails end up in the pots of the bird-catchers of the Gironde and Landes departments of France. More, perhaps, than ordinary conservationists they see that what happens off the reserve may be even more important to the welfare of the birds than a breeding season at peace. Observations may show that a habitat is used by different species at different times of year, but only ringing has shown that, even when a species is present throughout the year, individuals come and go: an entire population may imperceptibly move out and be replaced by another.

In the three-quarters of a century which have passed since the technique of bird ringing was invented it has spread to most countries of the world. From being a scientific novelty it has steadily grown to recognition as a basic scientific service, akin to a meteorological office or a geological survey, and is in some countries fully state-financed. It may not be generally known that in the last analysis all bird ringing in Britain is undertaken not merely by permission of, but actually on behalf of, the government, for the BTO is proud to have a service contract with the Natural Environment Research Council to provide a national bird-ringing service. This arrangement combines effectively two national traits: a willingness to find compromise solutions and a healthy respect for the contribution of the amateur. It is a blending of public and private enterprise which gets an important job done cheaply and well by harnessing the enthusiasms and expertise of ordinary men and women.

Page 125   Confined to extensive reed beds, the Reed Warbler proved
an ideal subject for a ringing project

Page 126 (above) A male Sparrowhawk sweeps from its nest with all the power and skill which makes it such a deadly killer in woodland; (below) a female Sparrowhawk plucks the foot of a small passerine to offer to her not over-enthusiastic young

Hawks and man

Ian Newton

The Sparrowhawk *Accipiter nisus* is found over much of Europe and Asia. It nests in woodland, and feeds on small birds. Formerly, in Britain it showed great stability in numbers, and bred with high success. But from the late 1940s it began to breed less well, and ten years later its population crashed. These unprecedented events were paralleled in Britain in the Peregrine *Falco peregrinus* and less markedly in some other species, and in continental Europe and North America in many predatory species (Ratcliffe 1970, Hickey 1969). They coincided with another unprecedented change, the release of certain poisonous and highly persistent chemicals into the environment, mainly for use in insect control. These were the organo-chlorine compounds, which include DDT, BHC and others, together with the cyclodienes, like aldrin, dieldrin and heptachlor.

Here I shall consider the extent of changes in breeding success and population in the Sparrowhawk in Britain, review the evidence for the involvement of the organo-chlorines, and the main lessons to be learned. An important part of the evidence consists of dating the changes precisely to find how closely they fit with organo-chlorine usage.

The Chemicals

DDT first came into use as an insecticide during the Second

World War, but only after 1946 was it used extensively in British agriculture, forestry and industry. The world over, it has remained the most effective chemical in many fields, especially against insects which carry human disease. It also enables people to grow cotton economically in some poor countries. The more toxic cyclodiene compounds were also used from about this date, but in Britain became widespread only after 1955, chiefly in seed-dressings. Over the same period, another group of chemically related compounds, the polychlorinated biphenols (PCBs) began to be used widely in plastics, paints, oils and other industrial products, from which they reached the environment.

These various chemicals are important because of their persistence—they last unchanged and active for many years after application—and also because they are soluble in fat. They can therefore accumulate in animal bodies, and pass from one organism to another, so that animals near the tops of food chains, like the Sparrowhawk, are especially liable to accumulate large concentrations. Study of the Sparrowhawk therefore gives some suggestion of what might happen to other animals if the use of such compounds was continued on a scale sufficient to increase environmental levels still further. In this sense the Sparrowhawk is perhaps a good indicator species, reflecting levels of these chemicals in the environment as a whole. The idea that an animal might be used to monitor pollution is not new and, as a parallel, canaries were used in coal mines years ago to indicate the deterioration in atmosphere caused by poisonous gases.

Restrictions

So far no restrictions have been placed on the use of DDT in Britain. But from 1962 the cyclodiene compounds were banned by voluntary agreement from dressings on spring-sown grain. These came as a result partly of public pressure arising from the thousands of pigeons and other birds found dead and dying around fields where dieldrin had been used. In 1966, dieldrin was also banned as a sheep dip, partly because it was found at substantial level in mutton intended for human consumption. From 1973, restrictions on all cyclodienes were extended to cover autumn-sown grain, but their limited use for other purposes continues. The latest government statistics indicate that, while the annual usage of DDT in Britain was about the same in the early 1970s as it was in the early 1960s, the use of the cyclodienes was reduced in this period by one-half. All the restrictions were voluntary, however, and as yet there is no legal comeback on people who ignore them.

Eggshell Thickness

From the late 1940s, it was noticed that nests of Sparrowhawks and Peregrines in Britain contained broken eggs on a scale hitherto unknown, and in circumstances that did not suggest predation. This led Ratcliffe (1970) to examine the shells, and to the important discovery that shells laid from this date were thinner than those laid earlier. From examination of more than 500 eggs, present in museums and private collections, the change in shells was dated precisely to 1947, the first year of widespread DDT usage, since which year it has persisted (see Table 1). The degree of thinning, moreover, was more marked in the intensely arable areas of south-east Britain than in the north-west, where DDT usage was less (Table 1). There was thus coincidence in both time and space between shell-thinning and the use of DDT.

TABLE I

Extent of change in Sparrowhawk egg-shells from different
regions of Britain. (From Ratcliffe 1970.)

| | Until 1946 | | From 1947 | | |
	No. eggs examined	Mean shell-index* (± se)	No. eggs examined	Mean shell-index* (± se)	Extent of change
South-east England	68	1·42 ± 0·01	129	1·12 ± 0·01	— 21%
Other regions	230	1·43 ± 0·01	150	1·23 ± 0·01	— 14%
All regions	298	1·42 ± 0·01	279	1·18 ± 0·01	— 17%

* Shell-index reflects relative weight and was calculated by the formula:
shell wt (mg)/shell length × breadth (mm).

Changes in Breeding Success

To assess the extent of changes in breeding success, it was
necessary to examine nesting before and during the time when
organo-chlorine pesticides were in widespread use. Details of
the former nesting success of Sparrowhawks were collated
from the diaries and notebooks of early naturalists, and from
the nest-record cards of the British Trust for Ornithology
(Newton 1974). By this last scheme, anyone who found a nest
could complete the details on a standard card, which was then
returned to a central collection to await analysis. All these data
were divided according to whether they were collected before
1947 (no organo-chlorines in widespread use); 1947–55
(DDT, BHC and related compounds, but practically no cyclodienes); and 1956–70 (DDT, BHC and related compounds
and cyclodienes). They were also subdivided according to
whether they referred to nests near farmland areas (within an
arbitrary 20km of farmland) or farther away. The assumption
was that birds nesting on farmland, where pesticide applications were heaviest, would have greater opportunity for
pesticidal contamination than would more distant ones. All
nests which failed through direct human intervention were
excluded.

TABLE 2
Proportion of Sparrowhawk nests producing young in different periods, excluding failures through direct human intervention.
(From Newton 1974.)

	No. clutches found before completion	No. (%) in which at least one egg hatched	No. (%) in which at least one young fledged	Causes of complete failure				Death of young
				Deserted eggs	Unhatched (incubated) eggs	Broken eggs	Unhatched and broken eggs	
Farmland								
Pre-1947	80	80 (100)	80 (100)	0	0	0	0	0
1947–55	29	19 (66)	19 (66)	0	1	8	1	0
1956–70	88	51 (58)	48 (55)	0	6	19	12	3
Non-farmland								
1956–70	20	19 (95)	19 (95)	1	0	0	0	0

Only nests which were found before laying had finished and which were followed to the end have been used in this table. The inclusion of nests found at later stages would have biased the sample in favour of success.

The results were clear cut (Tables 1 and 2). Before 1947, the success of Sparrowhawk nests in Britain which were not destroyed by human agency was extraordinarily high. In all the 80 for which a full record was obtained, at least one young was reared. Natural predation was lacking, presumably because the hen habitually stays near the nest before and throughout incubation, and drives away likely predators. On the Continent, the Goshawk *Accipiter gentilis* has been found to destroy many adult and nestling Sparrowhawks, but was absent from Britain at this time. In most nests in the sample, all the eggs hatched, and when an egg which failed to hatch was examined, it was invariably found to be addled (watery), with no obvious development. No instance was noted of young dead-in-shell; and egg breakage was extremely rare. Single eggs were broken in only two of 635 clutches seen. The high survival of nestlings was also striking, and in marked contrast to the situation in some other raptors. About 92 per cent of all young that hatched subsequently fledged, and in 78 per cent of broods all young survived. Some nests produced six fledglings.

Egg Breakage

Later results confirmed that a marked and significant decline in nesting success occurred on farmed areas of Britain from 1947. This was almost entirely due to an increase in egg breakages and in the failure of incubated eggs to hatch. No change occurred in the number of eggs laid and, once hatched, the young survived well. The frequency of egg breakage was about the same in 1947–55 as in 1956–70, but after 1955 there was a significant increase in the number of incubated eggs which failed to hatch. This was associated with the finding of many dead embryos in the later period (as well as more addled eggs). The implication is that, while shell-thinning and egg breakage occurred throughout the period of DDT usage, deaths of partly formed embryos came only after dieldrin and other cyclodienes came in.

How much did these changes reduce nesting success? Before 1947, in the absence of human intervention, every clutch could be expected to produce at least one young and the mean brood size was 4, on which basis 100 clutches produced 400 young. Under similar conditions in 1956–70, only 55 out of 100 clutches produced young, and the mean brood size in successful nests was 2·9. Thus 100 clutches produced only 160 fledglings, a 60 per cent drop from the pre-1947 level. This percentage is minimal, moreover, because it takes no account of non-breeding pairs, which have also increased in recent years. I came across no record of non-laying by established Sparrowhawk pairs before 1955, but during a study in southern Scotland in 1971–3 found that 49 out of 325 nests built were not laid in. Ratcliffe (1970) likewise found that 6 out of 19 nests seen in Cumberland in 1956–70 were not laid in, compared with 0 out of 38 before this date. Thus all the empty nests recorded were after 1955, so perhaps, like embryonic deaths, failure to lay also became widespread only after the cyclodienes came in. But the data are really too few to be sure.

No change in nesting success was apparent in the sample of nests situated more than 20km from arable land (Table 3). The proportion of pairs producing young, the hatching success, and the mean number of young per brood were about the same on such land in 1956–70 as in the whole country before 1947, and no egg breakages were recorded. Presumably the hawks in these areas met levels of organo-chlorines too low to influence their breeding significantly. The few analyses made of eggs from such areas confirm that the levels there were low.

Such remote areas, however, comprise only a small fraction of the land surface of Britain, and support only small numbers of Sparrowhawks.

TABLE 3

Clutch-sizes and brood-sizes in different periods.
(From Newton 1974.)

	Clutches		Broods	
	No. examined	Mean clutch-size	No. examined	Mean brood-size in successful nests
Farmland				
Pre-1947	635	4·8	117	4·1
1947–55	39	4·8	29	3·2
1956–70	46	4·9	219	2·9
Non-farmland				
1956–70	9	5·0	27	3·7

Care was taken to include only clutches not depleted by breakage, and broods in the last week before leaving.

Other Changes?

Many changes occurred on British farmland after 1946, as well as the dissemination of organo-chlorine pesticides. Hedgerows were removed, chemicals of other types were applied on increasing scale and, through greater mechanisation, operational procedures were changed. Some of these changes might also have influenced Sparrowhawk breeding. But these other changes occurred gradually over the period considered, not suddenly from 1946. Also, the breakage and non-hatching of eggs have been associated with contaminated and declining raptor populations in many parts of Europe and North America (Hickey 1969). In summary, the timing of shell-thinning and depressed nesting success in the Sparrowhawk, the restriction of failures to farmed areas, and the types of failure recorded, are consistent with the hypothesis that organo-chlorine compounds were the cause.

Organo-chlorine Levels in Eggs

An important part of the evidence for the involvement of these compounds in Sparrowhawk breeding comes from the demonstration that they are present in eggs, and that variations in the amounts present are correlated with variations in hatching success. Up to 1974, eggs from more than 500 Sparrowhawk nests, from many British counties, were analysed, and all were found to contain appropriate residues. The finding that there was little variation among eggs from the same clutch, yet wide differences between clutches, enabled Newton & Bogan (1974) to take for analysis single eggs from certain clutches, and then examine the success of the remaining eggs. In a Dumfriesshire area over three years, 325 nests were studied and eggs from 130 clutches were analysed.

The main residues found in these Scottish eggs were DDE (the principal metabolite of DDT), polychlorinated biphenols and dieldrin (in the bird's body, any aldrin is converted to dieldrin). Compared with 71 clutches collected in the same general area in 1945, these eggs showed an average reduction in shell thickness of 18 per cent. The extent of thinning in individual clutches, moreover, related to the amount of DDT in the eggs. In general the higher the DDE content the thinner the shell. Thinning was also correlated with the amount of PCB present, though less well, and only poorly with the amount of dieldrin. Since, of the three, only DDE has been shown experimentally to cause shell-thinning, the correlation of PCB with shell-thinning in our eggs was probably because the amount of PCB in eggs varied in parallel with the amount of DDE.

Among the 325 study nests, 110 (34 per cent) showed normal hatching success, 101 (31 per cent) showed partial

135

success, and 114 (35 per cent) failed completely. The criteria used to decide between normal, partial and nil success (in Table 4) were based partly on the hatching data collected in Britain before 1947, discussed above. The hatching success of these different clutches was then related to their organo-chlorine contents (Table 4). Those showing normal success had a lower mean residue level (157 ± 13ppm in lipid) than those showing partial success (mean = 226 ± 11ppm), and lower still than those showing nil success (293 ± 25ppm). In other words, the extent of breeding failure was associated with the amount of organo-chlorine residue in the eggs. It was also, as expected, related to the degree of shell-thinning.

TABLE 4

Hatching success[1] at Sparrowhawk nests in relation to organo-chlorine content and shell-indices of eggs

Success	Number of nests	Number from which egg analysed	Total organo-chlorine content (mean ppm ± se)	Shell-index (mean ± se)
Normal[2]	110	17	157 ± 13	1·27 ± 0·03
Partial[3]	101	74	226 ± 11	1·20 ± 0·01
Nil[4]	114	40	293 ± 25	1·11 ± 0·02

[1] Failures through direct human intervention are excluded.
[2] No more than one egg addled (watery), no breakage and no dead embryos.
[3] One or more eggs broken or with dead embryos, but at least one young hatched.
[4] No eggs hatched.

Causes of Failure

The main cause of unsuccessful breeding in this population was failure to lay, having built a nest. This occurred at 49 (15 per cent) of 325 nests, and accounted for 43 per cent of all complete failures. Egg breakage was the second commonest cause of failure, the 35 instances accounting for 11 per cent of all clutches and 31 per cent of all failures. Breakage was in general related to the degree of shell-thinning. Usually the eggs in a clutch were broken individually over several days, until only one remained which was then abandoned. Analyses of these remaining eggs from broken clutches gave organo-chlorine levels of 350 ± 47ppm. The third commonest cause of failure was desertion, which occurred at 5 per cent of all nests and accounted for 15 per cent of all failures. The clutches involved showed a wide range of organo-chlorine contents, with a mean of 200 ± 23ppm, lower than in the other types of complete failure. The remaining 13 clutches were unproductive because the eggs, though incubated and undamaged, failed to hatch. This involved 4 per cent of all nests and 11 per cent of all failures. Such failures might have been due to poor parental care, impaired gas and water exchange through a thin shell, or a direct toxic effect of high residue levels. Embryo deaths from thin shells alone seem unlikely, since the clutches involved had by no means the thinnest shells, but by far the highest organo-chlorine levels (mean 363 ± 19ppm). Among nests which produced at least one young, unhatched eggs were found in 51 (19 per cent of all nests), broken eggs in 27 (8 per cent of all nests), and both unhatched and broken eggs in another 23 (7 per cent of all nests). Once the eggs hatched, survival of young in all groups of nests was greater than 90 per cent.

Despite widespread shell-thinning, egg breakage was a less important cause of unsuccessful breeding than failure to lay, while desertions and embryo deaths also accounted for a large proportion of clutch failures. Clutches failing in these various ways, except desertions, showed organo-chlorine levels significantly higher than those showing normal success. This provided another strand of circumstantial evidence for the involvement of such compounds in Sparrowhawk breeding.

Population Trends

It is difficult to date the population crash precisely, even though it was widespread, because most bird-watchers noticed it only after it had happened. Several observers, however, were at that time keeping a regular annual check on a number of sites in different areas, and from their records it is possible to date the change more accurately. In intensely arable areas of south-east England (three observers), the first signs of a decline were noticed from the late 1940s, that is after DDT came into wide use but before the cyclodienes. In these and four other areas, however, a major crash came after 1955, dated by all seven observers between 1958 and 1960. After this the decline became evident to bird-watchers at large, as the species became almost extinct in south-east England and the Midlands. The crash was so sudden that it must have been due to the mass mortality of adult hawks, and not just their previous poor breeding. It is thus possible to link the first signs of a decline with DDT, in areas where the use of this material is likely to have been particularly heavy, and the major crash in the country as a whole with sudden and acute poisoning resulting from cyclodiene usage.

It was 3–4 years after the first restrictions in the cyclodienes in 1962 before much recovery was evident, but at the time of writing (1974) Sparrowhawks are again almost back to strength in many parts of the north-west, and though present, they are still much reduced in the south-east. Hence, the timing and geographical pattern of both the decline and the subsequent partial recovery followed closely the fluctuations and geographical pattern of such pesticide usage. The recovery occurred while nesting success was still depressed, which again implies that population changes were caused

138

more by changes in adult mortality than by changes in production of young. So far, the bodies of more than 100 Sparrow-hawks have been analysed at various laboratories, and all were found to contain a variety of organo-chlorines.

Experimental Evidence

All the evidence so far presented is circumstantial, based on correlations, and on coincidences in time and space between the extent of organo-chlorine usage and the extent of change in Sparrowhawk breeding and population. It is thus theoretically possible, but unlikely, that some other pollutant of which we are not yet aware has fluctuated in the environment and in animal tissues in exactly the same way as the organo-chlorines and caused these changes. But confirmation that the organo-chlorines could produce the effects observed in the wild came from feeding experiments in America. Shell-thinning, egg-breakage and embryo deaths occurred in both American Kestrels *F. sparverius* and Prairie Falcons *F. mexicanus* which were fed on diets containing DDT and dieldrin, but not in individuals of these same species fed on diets lacking these compounds (Porter & Wiemeyer 1969, Enderson & Berger 1970).

Conclusions

The several lines of evidence for the involvement of the organo-chlorines in the recent poor breeding of Sparrow-hawks and their population changes may thus be summarised. First, the shell-thinning and poor breeding were unprecedented within ornithological history, and likely to be linked with an unprecedented change in the environment. Second, shell-thinning closely followed the widespread use of

DDT, while the decline in population was associated with the introduction of the cyclodienes and the subsequent increase in population with the restrictions in cyclodienes. Third, the geographical pattern of these changes coincided with the pattern of pesticide usage, as both shell-thinning and population decline were most marked in the south-east where the amount of arable farming is greatest. Fourth, analyses of tissues and eggs showed these compounds to be present in all Sparrow-hawks and eggs examined in recent years. They were also found, at lower levels, in all the many prey species analysed (Prestt & Ratcliffe 1970). Fifth, the amount of residue in individual clutches was closely correlated with the success of those clutches. Together with the findings on the Peregrine and other species in the wild, and the experimental evidence mentioned above, the case for the involvement of the organo-chlorines in the Sparrowhawk's breeding and population changes becomes extremely compelling.

The fate of birds of prey like the Sparrowhawk is the proper concern of ecologists, but its indication of an important new environmental problem is of general concern. Recent research of this nature has shown that persistent organo-chlorine insecticides and PCBs are (a) biologically active at levels far lower than those that are lethal; (b) affecting populations far removed from areas of application; and (c) now widely distributed in soils, water and organisms throughout the world. Administrative action on the control of pesticide usage has usually taken these facts into account. But the extent to which any country can limit the use of organo-chlorines must obviously depend on local conditions. The need for at least some of their uses in tropical countries may continue for some time yet, but their total or partial withdrawal in the highly developed nations of the temperate zone seems a wise precaution to protect natural resources. The argument is not, as some

HAWKS AND MAN

have put it, whether one prefers birds to men, but whether men should take serious heed of what has happened to some birds as a result of using substances which are both valuable in controlling insects and at the same time dangerous to a wide range of other organisms. The need for caution and restraint in the use of persistent chemicals is perhaps the main lesson to be learned.

References

ENDERSON, J. H. & BERGER, D. D. 1970. 'Pesticides: eggshell thinning and lowered production of young in Prairie Falcons.' *Bio Science* 20: 355–6.

HICKEY, J. J. (ed). 1969. *Peregrine Falcon populations*. University of Wisconsin Press, Madison, Milwaukee & London.

NEWTON, I. 1974. 'Changes attributed to pesticides in the nesting success of the Sparrowhawk in Britain.' *J. appl. Ecol.* 11: 95–102.

NEWTON, I. & BOGAN, J. 1974. 'Organochlorine residues, eggshell thinning & hatching success in British Sparrowhawks.' *Nature* 249: 582–3.

PORTER, R. D. & WIEMEYER, J. N. 1969. 'Dieldrin & DDT effects on Sparrowhawk eggshells & reproduction.' *Science*, N.Y. 165: 199–200.

PRESTT, I. & RATCLIFFE, D. A. 1972. 'Effects of organochlorine insecticides on European birdlife.' *Proc. 15th Int. Orn. Congr.* pp 407–27.

RATCLIFFE, D. A. 1970. 'Changes attributed to pesticides in egg breakage frequency & eggshell thickness in some British birds.' *J. appl. Ecol.* 7: 67–107.

Between the tides

A. J. Prater

The meeting and merging of the sea with fresh water in an estuary provides one of the richest habitats for wildlife in Britain. Here birds and fish congregate to feed upon the vast numbers of small invertebrates which in turn extract the nutrients from the mud and water. Rivers bring down both fertilisers, leached from the soil, and organic materials, particularly sewage. At the estuary these materials mix with nutrients and small particles brought in from the sea by the tides. The pattern of tides, which continually varies in height, increases the diversity of plants in the estuary, for different species flourish under different inundation regimes.

Each to its Own

A quick search of an estuary soon reveals a series of habitats, each supporting its own characteristic wader populations. The mussel beds near the mouth of an estuary are used by Oyster-catchers, Turnstones and sometimes Purple Sandpipers; the sandy outer areas by Ringed Plovers and Sanderlings; the extensive muddy or sandy flats by flocks of Knot, Dunlin, Bar-tailed Godwit, Curlew and Grey Plover; and the muddy upper areas around the saltmarshes are where Redshank abound, together with less common species such as Greenshank, Spotted Redshank and Curlew Sandpipers during the autumn migration.

Page 143 (*above*) A young male Sparrowhawk caught bathing by a painstaking photographer; (*below*) before the BTO Estuaries Survey got under way only the population of Oystercatchers was at all well known because of its economic importance as a shellfish predator

Page 144 Widespread, numerous and common—but how many Curlew can be found in Britain? That is the sort of question asked by modern conservationists

Estuaries in Danger

Although many estuaries have not changed much during the last few hundred years, there has been a slow but steady loss which advanced technology is now accelerating and threatening to alter radically. From about the eighteenth century, marshlands associated with estuaries have been drained and saltmarshes reclaimed for agriculture; this has been particularly so on the eastern and southern coasts of England where rich silt deposits have been built up. At present the threats are threefold. Firstly, there is the natural threat of the chord grass *Spartina townsendii*. This hybrid form first colonised southern estuaries of England during the early 1900s, and has since spread rapidly into almost all estuaries where it is smothering the higher parts of the shore.

Secondly, and more important, are the industrial and commercial developments proposed for estuaries. These invariably involve the reclamation of parts of the shore, though the form the reclamation will take varies considerably. At present, industry is the largest threat, with an almost complete take-over of the once important mudflats at Teesmouth being the most advanced, though shore-based oil developments in Scotland and a revival of the third London Airport are still significant threats. Plans already exist for massive fresh-water reservoirs on the estuaries which are most important for waders in Britain, such as Morecambe Bay, the Wash and the Dee, while the advancement in reclamation techniques for agriculture also poses threats on the Wash. The need for leisure facilities has also, paradoxically, tended to destroy some of the very advantages of the peace of the estuaries. Yachting marinas have sprung up in many of the secluded creeks in the estuaries of south and east England, while waterskiing and power boats disturb roosting and feeding waders.

Thirdly, there is the threat from pollution, though its effect is as yet unknown. This threat seems likely to be an increasing one. The efficient control of effluents in the Thames and the Mersey has resulted in massive increases in the numbers of waders and ducks inhabiting those estuaries and perhaps indicates, if only indirectly, the effects which pollution must be having.

Top Estuaries for Waders

Counts have been made, in each month over the last five years, of the wader populations on British and Irish estuaries by the joint British Trust for Ornithology–Royal Society for the Protection of Birds–Wildfowl Trust 'Birds of Estuaries Enquiry' and the Irish Wildbird Conservancy 'Wetlands Enquiry'. These detailed counts have shown that our estuaries support hosts of waders. By adding together and then averaging the highest count of each species made in each year, it has been possible to draw up a list which shows the relative importance of each estuary—the 'top 20' estuaries.

TABLE 1

Top twenty estuaries for waders, Britain and Ireland

Morecambe Bay	234,000
Wash	177,000
Solway Firth	165,000
Dee	136,000
Ribble	133,000
Severn	72,000
Firth of Forth	66,000
Humber	56,000
Shannon/Fergus	56,000
Burry Inlet	40,000
Dundalk Bay	40,000

146

Strangford Lough	38,000
Lindisfarne	34,000
Foulness	31,000
Chichester Harbour	30,000
Duddon	29,000
North Bull	28,000
Langstone Harbour	27,000
Blackwater/Dengie	25,000
Swale	24,000

The waders which can be observed on British estuaries come from an enormous belt of the arctic, subarctic and north temperate regions of Canada, Greenland, Iceland, Scandinavia and the USSR. Those which breed in each part of this geographical zone can be divided into separate populations, each with its characteristic migration pattern and wintering area. Some of these populations can be separated by observers in the field, such as the small dark Ringed Plovers *Charadrius hiaticula tundrae* which breed in northern Scandinavia and the USSR. Other populations have distinct plumage characters which can be determined when trapped for ringing. A summary of the occurrence of the main population divisions of the most numerous species is set out below.

The waders of the breeding zones in north-east Canada and Greenland migrate into or through Europe. The Knot and Turnstone from there usually stop on the west coast of Iceland to refuel, while many of the Sanderlings and Ringed Plovers from Greenland probably make a direct and hazardous crossing of the North Atlantic Ocean. In contrast, the northern Scandinavian and Russian breeding birds are able to make a much less dangerous flight south and west along the shores of the Baltic Sea, stopping off for a few hours each day to feed at favourable areas such as at the Ottenby Bird Observatory in Sweden.

147

TABLE 2
Occurrence of wader populations, British Isles

	NE Canada	Greenland	Faeroes Iceland	Britain	W Europe S Scand	N Scand	USSR
Oystercatcher	—	—	PW	PW	PW	PW	W
Ringed Plover	—	P	P	PW	PW	P	P
Grey Plover	—	—	—	—	—	—	PW
Turnstone	PW	PW	—	—	—	P	P
Curlew	—	—	—	PW	PW	PW	—
Black-tailed Godwit	—	—	PW	PW	P	—	PW
Bar-tailed Godwit	—	—	—	—	—	P	—
Redshank	—	—	PW	PW	P	P	PW
Knot	PW	PW	—	—	—	—	PW
Dunlin	—	P	P	P	P	PW	PW
Sanderling	P	P	—	—	—	—	PW

P = Passage; W = Winter.

Massive Autumn Passage

Once these two streams of migrant waders reach the shores of western Europe, they intermingle in Britain and on the Waddenzee. At the height of the autumn migration, at the end of August or in early September, British estuaries support about 800,000 waders. Although waders are widespread on all estuaries at this time, a few areas are of particular importance. On the Wash up to 50,000 Dunlins and 4,000 Grey Plovers occur, on the Ribble over 80,000 Knots and 10,000 Bar-tailed Godwits have been recorded, while on Morecambe Bay 40,000 Oystercatchers, 20,000 Redshanks and 12,000 Curlews can be found. The Dee, too, with over 20,000 each of Oyster-catchers, Knots and Dunlins, is an important area in the autumn. The greatest variety of species is found during the autumn, when concentrations of over 150 Greenshanks have been seen on the Wash, the Blackwater and in Chichester Harbour, while on the Medway up to 250 Spotted Redshanks are regularly recorded.

During August and September many of the adult waders are moulting their wing feathers. Studies on the Wash have shown that most moulting waders have a low weight compared with non-moulting adults, indicating that those moulting are using their fat reserves to provide the energy needed to grow new feathers. Most of the waders using British estuaries as moult-ing grounds are those which will winter in Britain, Ireland and France. A proportion, especially of Dunlin and Grey Plover, will renew their flight feathers here before migrating south for the winter. Some populations of waders, particularly the southern Dunlins *Calidris alpina schinzii*, Scandinavian Turnstones and Ringed Plovers and Greenland Sanderlings, do not normally moult on British estuaries but pause briefly

149

to feed before moving south to their wintering grounds where they moult.

Passing Through

Many of the waders, particularly the young birds which occur in the autumn, move south to Iberia and West Africa for the winter. There is, however, a steady build-up in the total numbers of waders on our estuaries throughout the late autumn and early winter. Peak numbers are reached in January. These new arrivals are birds which have spent the autumn and moulted on the Waddenzee and have been forced westwards by the cold continental winter. Britain is fortunate to be the northernmost major wintering ground for waders in the world, as its climate is influenced by the warm North Atlantic Drift.

At the peak time up to $1\frac{1}{2}$ million waders winter in Britain and a further quarter of a million in Ireland, out of a total European population of 3 million. So Britain supports half of the European waders in winter, a fact that emphasises the considerable importance of our estuaries for these birds. During January international censuses have been carried out by the Wader Research Group of the International Waterfowl Research Bureau. These counts have shown that Britain has six of the top ten estuaries in Europe. These, in order of numerical importance, are: Morecambe Bay (179,000 waders), Wash (132,000), Solway Firth (105,000), Dee (73,000), Ribble (62,900) and the Firth of Forth (52,100). Of the main species of waders present, the 350,000 Knot represent 60 per cent of the European total, as do the 80,000 Redshank. Dunlin, with 550,000 wintering in Britain, Curlew (60,000) and Bar-tailed Godwit (43,000) each form half of the European population.

Mild Winters, More Waders

Since the severe winter of 1962–3, Britain has experienced a series of increasingly mild winters. The survival of species which are usually more southern in distribution, such as Grey Plover, Black-tailed Godwit, Spotted Redshank, Greenshank and Ruff, has been increased, with the result that the numbers of these wintering in Britain has been steadily rising. Of the last three species, which are still relatively uncommon, the numbers in Britain have now reached 100, 200 (with over twice this number in Ireland), and 1,200 respectively. The Ruffs have increased from less than 300 to 1,200 in just eight years and now flocks of 100 or more can usually be seen on the Solent, Ribble, Poole Harbour, Thames, Sussex coast near Pagham Harbour and on the Exe.

During early February the first of the British breeding Oystercatchers, Ringed Plovers and Redshanks, which have wintered within Britain, start to move back to their breeding territories. Estuarine habitats, particularly the outer sandy or shingle beaches, form a particularly important breeding area for Ringed Plovers. Although this species is widespread, the total English and Welsh population is of only just about 2,000 pairs, making it one of the less common breeding species. By the middle or end of March, most of the British nesters are back on territory. A parallel movement has been going on involving a return of Dunlin, Knot, Bar-tailed Godwit and Curlew to the Waddenzee.

Spring Build-up

By early April most of the wintering waders have left the estuaries for their breeding grounds, but some notable concentrations still occur. In Morecambe Bay between 80,000 and 100,000 Knot can be seen moulting into their chestnut-red summer plumage. Studies here have shown that they put on about 75gm of fat (about 55 per cent of their body weight) during a three-week period in April before departing to Iceland where they stop on their way to Greenland and Canada. There were over 71,000 Dunlin on the Wash in March 1974, mainly birds which had wintered elsewhere in Britain and were using the Wash as a gateway back to the continental coasts.

For a few weeks in late April and very early May there is a lull in the migration of waders through the estuaries, but suddenly—usually in the second week of May—a great influx of waders is seen on the west coast of Britain. These, mainly Dunlin, Ringed Plover and Sanderling, are found in considerable numbers on the few large estuaries around the Irish Sea; in particular, the Dee, the Ribble and Morecambe Bay, though some Welsh estuaries such as the Dyfi are also used. In eastern Britain this May passage is also discernible although the numbers involved are eclipsed by the western estuaries. These waders are ones which have wintered well to the south in Africa and are returning, using British estuaries as staging posts, to breeding grounds in Iceland, Greenland, and possibly Canada in the case of the Sanderling.

Many waders involved in this movement have been trapped, especially on the Wash, Dee and Morecambe Bay. It has been found that when they reach Britain their weight is low, but after they have fed for two to three weeks it has just about doubled. This fat deposit gives them the energy to fly straight to their breeding grounds. The distances covered and the speed of migration are instanced by a Sanderling which was ringed in South Africa in March and controlled on the Wash just two months (and 7,000 miles) later.

During the height of the spring passage, up to 13,000 Sanderling have been seen in Morecambe Bay, and 8,000 in both the Dee and Ribble estuaries. Ringed Plovers are not quite so numerous, though still abundant with 8,000 on Morecambe Bay and 3,000 on the Dee. Dunlins are the most numerous species, on Morecambe Bay 40,000 have been seen while both the Dee and Ribble may have up to 20,000 of them. Suddenly, as quickly as they arrived, they depart, usually at the end of May but sometimes, in a late season, not until early June. The departures usually occur on fine anticyclonic evenings, when the waders can be heard calling excitedly as they circle before heading north-west.

Summer Quiet

During the summer months of June and early July, relatively few waders remain on British estuaries. Most waders of Turnstone or Knot size and larger, do not breed until they are at least two years old. Many spend their first summer on the estuaries of Britain, and these birds choose the larger, more remote areas. The main concentrations (10,000 +) in Britain are on the Wash and the Ribble, though Morecambe Bay, the Solway Firth and the Firth of Forth often have fairly large numbers. Apart from these immature birds, the only waders to be seen on estuaries in the summer are the commonly breeding Ringed Plover, Redshank and Oystercatcher, or perhaps the rarer Dunlin or Black-tailed Godwit.

An assessment of the numbers of waders using the estuaries of Britain has been made possible by the BTO/RSPB/WT 'Birds of Estuaries Enquiry'.

TABLE 3

The highest monthly total of waders counted on
British estuaries, 1970–3

	Highest Count	Month of Highest Count
Dunlin	550,000	January
Knot	350,000	January
Oystercatcher	200,000	September and January
Lapwing	110,000	January
Redshank	103,000	September
Curlew	66,000	September
Golden Plover	55,000	January
Bar-tailed Godwit	43,000	January
Sanderling	26,000	May
Ringed Plover	25,000	August
Turnstone	13,000	January
Grey Plover	8,300	February
Black-tailed Godwit	5,300	September

The many threats to Britain's estuaries have already been noted. At the moment, few major schemes are under construction. The future, however, may not be so secure as an almost relentless pressure is being brought to bear on what remains of our unspoilt estuary shores. It is reassuring to note that in most instances to date there has been consultation, at an early stage, between the planning authorities and ornithological and other conservation bodies.

Detailed Studies

In recent years the Water Resources Board has initiated detailed studies on the waders in Morecambe Bay and the Wash and is doing so on the Dee. The need for studies in depth is amply illustrated by the results already obtained. For example, in both the Wash and Morecambe Bay the effect of developments would differ according to the siting and design of the reservoirs within each estuary and the effects would also be felt to differing degrees by the various species of waders present on the estuary. Some species, particularly Knot, Bar-tailed Godwit and Oystercatcher, have fairly precise feeding requirements. They also tend to move about to a considerable extent in search of their specialised food. This is particularly so of the Knot. Other species, such as Dunlin and Redshank, although apparently very flexible in the food they take, are extremely sedentary, moving little even between adjacent parts of the same estuary.

The major question to be answered is whether the feeding grounds likely to be left are sufficiently large to support the waders which may be displaced after development. Answers are not easy, and will vary from estuary to estuary, depending on the species present, their numbers and distribution, and the area where the development would take place. Indirect evidence is, however, beginning to accumulate which suggests that at some times of year, particularly in late winter, waders are normally under considerable stress under their present feeding regime. An increase in the numbers feeding on an area could bring, due to behavioural and spatial effects on both waders and their prey, a decrease in their food-obtaining efficiency. The waders, both those displaced and those already in the area, might then not obtain sufficient food to balance their expenditure of energy and perhaps starve.

Save the Estuaries

The importance of Britain's estuaries for wader populations is clear; it is equally clear that each estuary has only a limited area of intertidal flats. It is this feeding ground which is critical and once such an area is lost, it can never be recovered. It is therefore essential that long-term planning should take place to ensure that enough of this unique and valuable habitat is conserved. It should not be forgotten that several of our estuaries are amongst the most important estuaries in the world for wading birds. This is an incalculable asset which should not unthinkingly be destroyed.

Contributors

Peter Conder   Peter is the Director of the Royal Society for the Protection of Birds which, under his leadership, has grown from a small society into a national organisation of strength and significance. Yet he retains a passion for birds, for the countryside and for, perhaps, a less desk-bound existence.

John A. Burton   John is a natural history writer specialising in conservation. He was assistant Editor of *Birds of the World* and now works actively as Natural History Consultant to Friends of the Earth and as editor of the International Council for Bird Preservation's magazine *Birds International*. He has written several books, and numerous articles on a variety of natural history topics.

M. D. England   Derrick is at the top of his craft as a bird photographer and has a special bent towards rare and difficult species. He was the first to photograph the Great Bustard on the nest, the first to photograph Black-winged Kites in Europe and now continues his search on a worldwide basis. He has an OBE following a highly successful hospital career.

John Gooders   Our editor, formerly a schoolmaster and college lecturer, is now a professional writer about birds. He has written the definitive guides *Where to Watch Birds* and *Where to Watch Birds in Europe*, both recently revised, and edited the mammoth 9-volume *Birds of the World*. Other titles include *Wildlife Photography* (with Eric Hosking), *Wildlife Paradises, Birds—a Survey of the Bird Families of the World*, and he is currently engaged on a *World Guide to Birds* for David & Charles.

Kenneth Williamson   After spending the war in the Faeroe Islands, Ken was Director of the Fair Isle Bird Observatory until 1956. He joined the British Trust for Ornithology in 1958 and is now their Populations Research Officer. He is editor of *Bird Study* and has written books on several islands and island groups in the north-east Atlantic for which he has an enduring passion.

C. Hilary Fry   Hilary works in the thriving Zoology Department at the University of Aberdeen. He was formerly based in Africa south of the Sahara, where his main interest was in the migration of small passerines across the desert to the north. He was a member of the trans-African hovercraft expedition.

M. P. Harris   Degrees at the University College of Wales, Swansea, led Mike to the Edward Grey Institute of Field Ornithology where he continued his studies of seabirds, with long spells overseas mainly in the Galapagos. He is one of the leading authorities on his chosen bird group, and now works for the Institute of Terrestrial Ecology on Puffins and other seabirds in Scotland.

Bryan Nelson   Bryan is another seabird expert with an impressive clutch of papers to his credit. He is particularly interested in gannets and boobies having started his career

158

by working on the behaviour of the North Atlantic Gannet, and continued by studying each of the other Sulidae in turn. He now works in the Zoology Department of the University of Aberdeen and is the author of books on the Galapagos and the oasis of Azraq.

Robert Spencer   Bob has been running the national ringing scheme for the British Trust for Ornithology for more years than he cares to remember. He has been Secretary-General of EURING, the European Committee for Bird-ringing, since 1963.

Ian Newton   After working on the British finches, Ian turned his attention to the birds of prey with the same calm and dispassionate eye of the professional scientist. The result is a fuller understanding of these birds and the effects that man has had on them over the years.

A. J. Prater   Tony Prater joined the British Trust for Ornithology at a time when pressure on our estuaries was rising to a peak. It has been his job to find out just how many birds use the inter-tidal zones of Britain, and to liaise with others overseas to build up a picture of waders along the Atlantic flyway.

Bird books from Newton Abbot

1. David & Charles

Our current catalogue includes about twenty bird titles, ranging from Tony Soper's famous guide to food and shelter for wild birds, *The New Bird Table Book*, £2·50 (illustrated by Robert Gillmor) to the exhaustive *Parrots of the World*, £35·00—the definitive text by Joseph M. Forshaw and numerous colour plates by William T. Cooper ensure that the book will become a scarce collectors' item of antiquarian value.

Tony Soper is co-author with John Sparks of two books on individual species, also illustrated by Robert Gillmor, *Owls*, £3·50 and *Penguins* £4·50. Other definitive single-species studies include Colin R. Tubbs's *The Buzzard*, £5·50, John A. G. Barnes's *The Titmice of the British Isles* £5·25 (dealing fully with the habits of tits as they affect humans, for example opening milk bottle tops) and Sylvia Bruce Wilmore's *Swans of the World*, £5·25. A good introduction for younger readers is Peter Goodfellow's *Projects With Birds*, £2·95, while bird lovers of all ages will enjoy the anthology edited by Bruce and Margaret Campbell *The Country-man Bird Book*, £3·95.

Hugh Brandon-Cox's *Summer of a Million Wings*, £4·50, vividly describes the arctic quest for the sea eagle, while the fascinating story of the world's migratory sea birds is told in a brilliant text by R. M. Lockley illustrated with colour and black-and-white pictures in the handsome *Ocean Wanderers*, £5·25. R. M. Lockley is also author of the volume on Wales in our 'Regional Naturalist' series.

Write to David & Charles, Newton Abbot, for a free copy of our seasonal catalogue or send 25p for our complete catalogue. Prices quoted here are correct from August 1975–January 1976.

2. Readers Union

The Country Book Club and The Country Book Society, two of the Readers Union Group of Book Clubs, both include a wide variety of books on birds. The Country Book Club provides a monthly book reprinted at bargain prices especially for members; the emphasis is on a good read, and members normally buy at less than a third of the cost of the original edition. The Country Book Society offers a wider selection including reference titles such as field guides: members are only asked to choose at least four titles from the dozens they are offered each year. Send £5 to Readers Union, Newton Abbot, to start your membership of either Club.